ROYAL COMMISSION ON HISTORICAL MONUMENTS
ENGLAND

YORK

Historic Buildings

in the
Central Area

A Photographic Record

LONDON · HER MAJESTY'S STATIONERY OFFICE

ISBN 0 11 700912 1

CONTENTS

iii

LIST OF PLATES

(The numerals in brackets refer to the Monument numbers in the complete Inventory. The positions of the Monuments are shown on maps following p. 24. Numerals in the margins on pages 1–24 refer to the plate numbers.)

iv

PREFACE

This book derives from the fifth volume (1981) of the Royal Commission's *Inventory* of monuments in the City of York. The series began with two specialised volumes (1962, 1972) dealing respectively with the Roman period and the medieval defences of the city. The third volume (1972) was devoted to monuments of all periods in the area of the city to the south-west of the River Ouse and the fourth volume (1975) likewise covered the north-eastern part of the city outside the city walls. The fifth volume deals with the central area where many of the principal buildings are situated, and the sixth and final volume will be entirely devoted to York Minster.

These volumes, which record all buildings and other structures erected before 1850, contain much detailed description and are inevitably expensive. In order to make a selection of the most significant material in the fifth volume available to a wider public this shorter version has been produced. It includes all the 200 pages of plates from the full volume, and has a specially written introduction which discusses many aspects of the whole range of buildings illustrated, but its contents are based on the fifth York *Inventory* alone.

Of 539 buildings mentioned in the full volume, 161 are illustrated in this book. The photographs are arranged in the following sequence. After several pages of early sketches and general views of streets, there is a substantial section devoted to parish churches and their fittings. The next section deals with public and institutional buildings, followed by a small group of outstanding houses of the Georgian period. The final sections cover medieval timber-framed buildings and smaller houses of the 17th to 19th centuries. The Roman remains in the central area, the City Walls, York Castle and the Minster are not included in this book since they are treated in other volumes of the *Inventory*. It must be emphasised that most of the buildings illustrated are private property, though some of the churches and major buildings are normally open to the public.

The introduction has been written by Mr. D. W. Black, B.A., F.S.A., one of the Commission's Principal Investigators, who has drawn on much material prepared by all of the Commission's staff who worked in the city. The photographs were mostly taken by Messrs. T. H. E. Buchanan and C. J. Bassham; Mrs. J. Bryant has assisted with the editorial work.

The Commission's survey of central York could not have been accomplished without the co-operation of many people, including numerous owners and occupiers who generously allowed access to their buildings. A full list of acknowledgements appears in the *Inventory*.

June, 1981   P. J. Fowler, *Secretary to the Commission*

YORK

HISTORIC BUILDINGS
IN THE CENTRAL AREA

The area covered by this book is the central part of York, within the medieval city walls and on the north-east bank of the River Ouse. It includes the whole of the site of the Roman legionary fortress founded in AD 71, a strip of land lying to the south-west of the fortress between it and the Ouse, and a much larger area to the south-east crossed by the River Foss. In the present day, the area is divided naturally into two parts by the Foss; the larger one is the central core proper, with the civic buildings and the principal shopping streets, and the other is to the south-east of the Foss, where virtually all development before modern times was in the street of Walmgate which runs in an almost direct line from Foss Bridge to Walmgate Bar.

The street pattern has its origin in the Roman plan and Petergate and Stonegate follow, with slight deviations, the lines of the *via principalis* and *via praetoria* of the fortress. Much of the rest of the present plan was probably well established before the Norman Conquest, and many of the streets still have names of Scandinavian origin. After the Conquest the Castle was established, cutting across the main road to the south which had followed a line from Castlegate to Fishergate, and the Foss was dammed to form the King's Fish-pond. Fire devastated the city in 1069 and again in 1137. Few documents and fewer buildings survive from the period before the second fire. From the later part of the 12th century, however, numerous title deeds have been preserved naming, in the whole city, forty streets and thirty-five parish churches.

The medieval street plan survived with little alteration until the early 19th century. The map **1** published in Edward Baines' *Directory* of 1822 shows that the principal open spaces were the old market places at St. Sampson's Square and Pavement, and the latter had been enlarged by the demolition of the chancel of All Saints' Church in 1782. St. Helen's Square, the true civic centre **2** of York, with the Mansion House on the south-western side, was then even smaller than it is now.

The revised edition of the map published in 1847 showed considerable changes. Parliament Street, the largest single redevelopment scheme in central York, had been created in 1835 by the clearance of all the buildings between St. Sampson's Square and Pavement to provide a new and extensive market place. About the same time St. Leonard's Place, with the sweeping curve of its stuccoed **154** terrace, had been formed by removal of part of the city wall thus allowing new and easier access to the city centre which avoided the bottleneck of Bootham Bar. A row of houses fronting Petergate had been pulled down to allow a better view of the west front of the Minster, a process completed later in the century when Duncombe Place (previously Lop Lane) was widened by the total demolition of all houses on its south-east side, and an open vista was created as far back as Museum Street.

In spite of severe losses, York still retains a wealth of historic buildings from medieval times onwards. Though the parish churches have been depleted in number only Norwich among the great medieval cities of England retains more. The appearance of pre-Georgian York is best preserved in streets such as Low Petergate or the Shambles; the latter is now one of the chief tourist attractions **125, 124** of York but it is only in relatively modern times that this narrowest of city streets has been thought to be remarkable or attractive. Other streets were widened in the 18th and 19th centuries, such as Church Street in 1835, and elsewhere a greater spaciousness was achieved by the cutting back of overhanging jetties of timber-framed houses and their replacement by brick facades built upright from the ground.

Parish Churches

York, like other major medieval cities such as London, Norwich, Winchester and Lincoln, possessed a large number of parish churches, many of them fairly small. Of the medieval churches in the central area, fourteen survive in whole or in part though most are no longer in use for regular worship. Redundancy is not only a modern problem; eight churches were closed in the 16th century and subsequently demolished. Another two, St. Crux and Holy Trinity, King's Square, have been demolished in more recent times. However, St. Andrew's, which was utilised for a variety of purposes after its 16th-century redundancy, has returned to religious use and is now a meeting house of the Christian Brethren.

Little is known about the early churches in the central area. The recent excavation of the site of St. Helen-on-the-Walls in Aldwark has revealed a probable 10th-century origin, and carved stone fragments found in or near St. Denys', All Saints, Pavement, St. Sampson's and St. Crux suggest that there were pre-Conquest churches on these sites. The only standing remains certainly of pre-Conquest date are at St. Mary, Castlegate; much of the walling around the chancel arch is 11th-century and shows that the church was clearly of substantial size. A gable probably of the 11th century is preserved in the east wall of St. Cuthbert's but otherwise the earliest surviving work in central area churches is of 12th-century date. Foremost are two Norman doorways at the churches of St. Denys and St. Margaret, both in Walmgate. That at St. Denys' would originally have been to the nave but this was demolished in 1797 and the doorway, clearly still valued at that time for its wealth of carving, was reset on the south aisle of the former chancel. The five orders of the archway are carved with foliage decoration, beakheads, chevron ornament and a variety of other motifs. Inside the church are several 12th-century grotesque corbel heads.

The doorway at St. Margaret's is also reset. It was brought from the church of St. Nicholas' Hospital outside Walmgate Bar, the largest of the four extramural leper hospitals of York, which was already in existence in the 1150s but had been ruined during the siege of the city in 1644. The arch has four orders and the voussoirs are carved with representations of the Labours of the Months, Signs of the Zodiac, mythological beasts, and other subjects.

The early York churches were probably simple unaisled buildings, as excavations have shown St. Helen, Aldwark, to have been and as the existing remains at St. Mary, Castlegate, appear to indicate. By the late 12th century there was an aisled church at St. Michael, Spurriergate. The arches were rebuilt at a higher level in the 15th century and the original waterleaf capitals reset. At the same time the west tower was built; this stands within the body of the church and has remarkable piers and capitals in 12th-century style which match those of the original arcades, a most unusual medieval example of historicism. The external appearance of the church was completely altered in 1821 when the east and south walls were rebuilt in gritstone, a material not used much in York parish churches in the Middle Ages except when reused Roman material was employed. No old sketches or views of St. Michael's are known and its appearance before the 19th century can only be conjectured.

At St. Mary, Castlegate, a north aisle was added in the 12th century and though the arches were rebuilt later, piers with scalloped capitals, a typical Norman form, remain. A south aisle was added in the early 13th century. Little work from that century survives in churches in the central area and, though there is evidence of much building activity in the 14th century, no churches retain enough for them to be considered as prime examples of the period.   15

All Saints, Pavement, was recorded in Domesday and some evidence exists that work was done there in the 12th century, but in the 14th century it was rebuilt on a spacious scale with aisles throughout. A west tower was built in the 15th century, standing within the body of the church and flanked by aisles as is common elsewhere in York. The tower is surmounted by an octagonal lantern with large openings in each face, a prominent and distinctive feature of the city centre. The chancel and its aisles, being dilapidated, were demolished in 1782. Much of the exterior was refaced in the 19th century and the north aisle wall rebuilt in a different form without buttresses.   12

Another church which has been altered by partial demolition is *St. Denys'* in Walmgate. Unlike All Saints', the aisled chancel survives and now forms the whole church, the nave having been pulled down in 1798, the year after its west wall collapsed. The church is now much wider than it is long, the arcades being only of two bays. The north aisle is of 14th-century date and the rest of the church is of the 15th century except for the tower which was built in 1847.   11

St. Margaret's, also in Walmgate and not far from St. Denys', has already been mentioned for the reset Norman doorway brought from St. Nicholas'. Though a church is known to have been on this site by the 12th century, the main part of the existing church was built in the 14th century. The tower, largely of brick, was built in 1684–5 to replace one that had fallen a few years earlier, and in 1851–2 the north aisle was rebuilt and the old part of the church restored.   11

St. Helen's is a relatively small church which has been much restored but is prominent because it stands in the very centre of the city, on one side of St. Helen's Square, opposite the Mansion House. The exterior is mostly of the mid 19th century, though it repeats what was there before as sketched by Buckler in 1814. There is evidence of a church on the site in the 12th century and that an aisle may have been added to it in the 13th century. The south arcade was built in the 14th century, but in the next century the whole church seems to have been very much altered; it was at this time that the octagonal lantern, which is the most conspicuous feature of the church, was added.   13 2 17

Holy Trinity, Goodramgate, is another church with a complex development and retains traces or substantial elements of every century from the 12th to the 15th. An inconspicuous church in a secluded churchyard, it is now celebrated for its interior which escaped modernisation in the Victorian period. The box-pews of various shapes and sizes that fill the nave and aisles are mainly of the 18th century but incorporate some 17th-century work. The south wall of the church has 14th-century windows each of three lights with reticulated tracery under a straight head; when the Chapel of St. James was built further to the south in the early 15th century, two windows of this type which had been displaced from the south aisle were reset in the new chapel.   9 16 24

It was in the 15th century that the architecturally most accomplished churches were built in York. The largest is *St. Mary*, Castlegate, now an exhibition centre. Inside, the structure of the arcades of the nave and chancel is of many dates, the result of a long development from the 11th century onwards. The exterior is almost wholly of the 15th century though it is the product of more than one building campaign. The buttressed and pinnacled walls of the aisles have large square-headed windows with thin tracery though one on the north side is of the 14th century, perhaps reset because   14 15 24, 25 of the stained glass it then contained. It was possibly connected with the Northfolk chantry which is believed to have been in this part of the church. The west end of the nave represents a different stage of rebuilding and is contemporary with the tower, which is the most prominent feature of the church. The spire, 154 feet high, stands on a tall octagonal drum.

2 Two 15th-century churches of impressively unified design were St. Crux and St. Martin-le-Grand. *St. Crux*, in Pavement, was dedicated in 1424. Architecturally it was of a high order with an outstanding group of fittings and monuments. The tower, at the west end of the south aisle, was rebuilt in 1697 and the whole church was demolished in 1887. A church hall on a smaller scale was erected **9** on the site out of some of the old materials. *St. Martin's* in Coney Street, built in the second quarter **19** of the century, was seriously damaged in an air raid in 1942 and is now a ruin except for the south aisle. Both this church and St. Crux illustrate the late medieval tendency to eliminate the chancel as a separate structural entity, with the nave clerestorey carried through unbroken to the east end. The **25** surviving aisle of St. Martin's, with its fine Perpendicular windows, displays two local design characteristics: the pierced crenellated parapet, and buttresses projected upwards as narrow pinnacles connected to the wall by carved gargoyles.

Two other 15th-century churches of similar form, aisled and without separate chancels, are *St.* **10, 12** *Sampson's* and *St. Saviour's* but both were almost wholly reconstructed in the middle of the 19th **20** century. *St. Andrew's*, the only one of the churches made redundant in the 16th century of which the fabric survives, was a small church with unaisled nave and chancel. It has suffered much from the **10** vicissitudes of time and has been partly rebuilt in brick. *St. Cuthbert's* in Peasholme Green is another unaisled 15th-century church, though of exceptional width. The east wall contains the gable end of a much earlier building, probably of the 11th century, and there are indications that there was a structure, perhaps for a vestry, further to the east. Internally, there is an impressive ceiled roof in the form of a barrel-vault.

13 The last medieval church to be built in York was *St. Michael-le-Belfrey*, standing close to the Minster. Designed by the cathedral master mason John Forman it was completed in 1537 though, like all the city centre churches, stands on the site of an earlier building. The west front was rebuilt **25** in 1867 as a close though not exact copy of the previous front but the side walls with windows with **19** ogee-headed lights remain unaltered except for some renewal of masonry. The six-bay interior is spacious and well-lit from a tall clerestorey. The architectural detailing is more elaborate than is **27** general in city churches, with moulded arches and high bases to the shafted piers.

Apart from nonconformist chapels, the only new church building in the 19th century was for the **13** revived Roman Catholic hierarchy. *St. George's* in the Walmgate area was designed by the local architect Joseph Hansom, who was to become one of the leading architects of Catholic churches in the Victorian era, and opened in 1850. Fully aisled and without a clerestorey it is very much in the York tradition and takes its name from the medieval church of the same dedication which stood nearby.

PRE-CONQUEST STONES

Only two carved stones in the area, outside the Minster, can be attributed to a date before the Danish **21** invasion. Both were found on the site of St. Leonard's Hospital and are fragments of cross-shafts. One has a memorial inscription and the other an inhabited vine scroll on the main face as well as other scrollwork and interlace.

The other carved stones date from a later period, within the century before the Norman Conquest. From St. Mary, Castlegate, are several fragmentary cross-heads. One is a wheel-head cross, the faces **22** of which are carved with bosses, beasts and interlace, with much use also made of pellet and cable ornament; another has a representation of the Crucifixion. A cross-shaft fragment, found in 1963 during building work at 6 Newgate, is of magnesian limestone, a material not much used at this period when gritstone was preferred. Stylistically this fragment differs from other examples con- **23** sidered here, and its closest parallel is the Nunburnholme Cross. Each face has an arched panel: one is carved with a haloed head and the other three with entwined beasts. Two coped grave-slabs, from All Saints, Pavement, and St. Denys', are carved with entwined animals, and a flat slab, also from **23, 21** St. Denys', has single-ribbon interlace.

The damaged dedication stone at St. Mary, Castlegate, is of the greatest importance in that it **21** records the building of the church by Efrard, Grim and Aese, though the date is unfortunately missing.

CHURCH FURNITURE AND FITTINGS

Craftsmanship in wood in church furnishing is mainly represented by the communion table and its immediate surroundings such as communion rails and reredos. Many communion tables were installed in the 17th century to replace medieval stone altars, and examples survive at All Saints, **35** Pavement, St. Cuthbert's and St. Michael's. They are of simple but sturdy construction with stout, turned legs and a limited amount of decoration on the rails, such as fluting on the one at St. Cuthbert's. York is notable for several sets of communion rails which enclose the communion table on three sides, with a central pair of gates projecting boldly forward on a semicircular plan. Some of this type were destroyed in the 19th century but almost contemporary examples survive at St. Michael-le-Belfrey of 1712 by William Etty, and nearby at Holy Trinity, Goodramgate, made in 1715 by John **34** Headlam. There is also a good set of rails with carved balusters, though without the curved gates, at **38** St. Michael, Spurriergate. At this church is an early 18th-century reredos with fluted pilasters, round- **37** headed panels bearing the Lord's Prayer, Creed and Decalogue and, surmounting the whole com- position, a carved figure of St. Michael slaying the dragon. At St. Michael-le-Belfrey is an even more splendid reredos with detached Corinthian columns over which the entablature breaks forward; **37** it is contemporary with the communion rails and made by the same craftsman.

Among several 17th and 18th-century pulpits, the most outstanding is at All Saints, Pavement, **36** with a sounding-board dated 1634 on the soffit. Another fine piece of wood carving is the font cover at St. Martin, Coney Street, dated 1717, one of several of similar type in York. Of a number of **36** examples of painted panels bearing the Royal Arms, the earliest, dated 1669, is in the chapel of the **32** Merchant Adventurers' Hall. Others are at All Saints, Pavement, and St. Helen's.

There are several 15th-century doors: those at St. Cuthbert's, St. Sampson's and St. Crux (rehung **26, 158** in the church hall) have vertical ribs and tracery, resembling the pattern of contemporary windows. Doors at the Merchant Taylors' Hall and St. William's College are generally similar, but being in a secular context have inset wickets. Of exceptional importance is the Romanesque closing-ring on the **33** door of All Saints, Pavement, with the ring held by a beast's head; it has been reset and the back-plate is now fixed to a 17th-century door.

All York churches, even those now redundant, retain several bells. A few survive from the medieval period but most date from the 17th and 18th centuries, when York was an important centre for bell-founding, with the two families of Smith and Seller predominant. One notable peel, not now hung,

39 is at St. Michael, Spurriergate; made in 1681 by Samuel Smith senior for the Minster it was taken to the church in 1765.

BRASSES AND MONUMENTS

For a city of the importance of York, the surviving medieval brasses are disappointing. No figure brasses survive though several were recorded in the 17th century and a number of indents remain. Small plates with black-letter inscriptions in Latin include one of 1458 to Thomas Danby in Holy **40** Trinity, Goodramgate, and another in St. Michael, Spurriergate, to William Wilson who died in 1517. A late 16th-century example in similar style, though in English, is to Thomas Colthurst in St. Martin, Coney Street. By the 17th century, lettering was normally in capitals as on the brass of Christopher Harington in St. Martin's which also has a half-length figure, and arms of the Goldsmiths' Company. Another half-length figure is that of Robert Askwith in All Saints, Pavement, although the inscription which existed in the early 18th century is now lost.

Apart from floor-slabs with simple marginal inscriptions no medieval monuments survive in the **41** central area except for some in the Minster. From the early 17th century, the Watter monument in St. Crux, with recumbent effigies, is the only one of its kind in a York parish church. Figure sculpture **42** of the same period occurs on the monument of Dorothy Hughes in St. Denys' with the deceased **41** kneeling in prayer, and as portrait busts on the Sheffield monument of 1633 in St. Martin, Coney **44** Street. From subsequent periods the finest effigies are those of Robert and Priscilla Squire standing proud and self-assured on their early 18th-century monument in St. Michael-le-Belfrey.

Cartouches are a common form of wall-monument in the late 17th and early 18th centuries. That **42** to Mary Woodyeare of 1728 in St. Michael-le-Belfrey has a curved surface and was originally fixed to one of the piers in the church. Charles Mitley's 1758 memorial in St. Cuthbert's is unusually late for a cartouche, but Mitley, a carver, may have made it himself some years earlier. A late 17th-century **43** monument with an unusual conceit is that of Roger Belwood in St. Crux; on the inscription tablet he is remembered as 'a learned man', and this is echoed by representations of piles of books to each side. On another monument in St. Crux, of half a century later, the former career of Sir Tancred Robinson is symbolised by naval trophies.

From *c.*1770 onwards until well into the 19th century monumental sculpture in York was dominated by the Fisher family. Their best work is generally of before 1800, in a refined neoclassical idiom and often using coloured marbles. The wall-monument to William Hutchinson in **43** St. Michael, Spurriergate, is a good example of their style; that to Henry Waite in St. Crux is rather less typical, with a medallion containing a portrait in profile.

STAINED GLASS

The city of York contains the greatest concentration of medieval stained glass in England. Much of this is in the Minster but that in the parish churches is exceptional by the standards of other cities in the country. The survival in York of so much medieval glass has usually been ascribed to the firm control exercised by Lord Fairfax as Governor of the city after the siege in 1644, and there is a tradition that he took the glass out of the windows to protect it. It should not be forgotten, however, that the glass had already survived the period of equal if not greater destruction during the Reformation in the previous century.

The medieval glass is to be found principally in six churches: All Saints, Pavement, Holy Trinity,

Goodramgate, St. Denys', St. Martin, Coney Street, and the two churches dedicated to St. Michael. There are small amounts at St. Mary, Castlegate, and St. Helen's and some fragments at St. Cuthbert's.

The only 13th-century glass surviving in a parish church is at St. Denys' and consists of small coloured medallions containing figure-subjects set within a monochrome field of naturalistic **55** grisaille. Two of the roundels have been identified as scenes from the story of Theophilus, the only glass depicting this subject in York. The 14th-century glass in St. Denys' includes three windows in **60** the north wall with figures of saints. In the east window of St. Michael-le-Belfrey is reset glass of **49** mid 14th-century date including scenes from the life of Our Lord assembled from more than one window but presumably all from the earlier church. The paucity of glass from the second half of the 14th century is probably due to mortality from the Black Death among patrons and glass-painters alike. The recovery from this, near the end of the century, is illustrated by the series of Passion scenes now in All Saints', which shows a new vitality and provides many interesting iconographical **48, 50** details.

The Jesse window in St. Michael, Spurriergate, is of the early 15th century. After being badly **52, 53** jumbled for several centuries, glass of excellent quality has been revealed by restoration. It probably overlapped chronologically and has some similarities with the great east window in York Minster, made by John Thornton in 1405–8. An adjoining window in St. Michael's dates from the middle of the 15th century and contains eight panels depicting the Nine Orders of Angels. This was a popular **52, 53** theme in York and occurs also in St. Martin, Coney Street, in the former west window which had fortunately been removed for safety before the bombing of 1942. Now reset in the north wall of the reduced church, the subject appears in the tracery lights, expanded to ten orders to suit the symmetry **54** of the stonework. This window was given by the vicar, Robert Semer, just before his death in 1443, and the donor himself is depicted; the theme of the window is the life of St. Martin of Tours, which **54** is illustrated by a number of haphazardly-arranged scenes. Although the colouring and general **56, 61** effect are good, the draughtsmanship shows a distinct deterioration from previous standards.

The second half of the 15th century provides two other notable windows. The east window of St. Denys', made between 1452 and 1455, contains a central Crucifixion flanked by the Virgin and **47** St. John. The east window of Holy Trinity, Goodramgate, was given by the rector, John Walker, **45** in 1471 and exhibits painting of excellent quality. The subject matter includes the Corpus Christi **46** (with a very similar composition to the same subject in St. Martin's), St. George, St. Christopher, St. John the Baptist and the Virgin Mary. The Corpus Christi Guild and the Guild of St. Christopher **57** and St. George were the two most important guilds in York and the donor was an important official in them. There is also an interesting Coronation of the Virgin with the three persons of the Trinity **58** portrayed as similar figures wearing imperial arched crowns. This window originally had two additional rows of panels at the bottom, one of which contained five representations of the Virgin, each in a rayed mandorla. In the 18th or 19th century some of these figures were moved to the east **55** window of the north aisle.

The last examples of medieval glass are to be found in St. Michael-le-Belfrey, dating from between 1525, when rebuilding of the church was started, and *c.* 1540. The large single figures, strong in colour but weak in draughtsmanship, are more interesting historically than artistically. The small panels of the Thomas Becket series, more of which are in the Minster, are a noteworthy addition to **49, 63** the iconography of that saint.

The post-Reformation glass is, as might be expected, mostly secular in character. In the second half of the 17th century the Gyles family kept the craft alive, and most of the surviving panels are probably by Henry Gyles who maintained an acceptably high standard and work signed by him survives at the Merchant Taylors' Hall. A window incorporating the Stuart Royal Arms, now in the Victoria and Albert Museum, is undoubtedly by him but is not, as was previously thought, the former west window of the Guildhall, removed in 1862. After the death of Henry Gyles in 1709 the continuity of glass-painting in the city was interrupted for many years until it was revived by William Peckitt. He was perhaps the foremost English artist in this medium in the later 18th century and supplied glass to many other places as far afield as Oxford and Exeter. His draughtsmanship, especially of faces, was weak but his feeling for design and, in particular, abstract patterns was consistently good. He was responsible for a window formerly at 35 Stonegate and now in the City Art Gallery and another work almost certainly by him is the stair window at 9 New Street.

NONCONFORMIST CHAPELS AND MEETING HOUSES

Though of much later date than the parish churches, dissenting chapels in the city centre have suffered just as much from redundancy and very few are still in use for worship. The earliest surviving is the *Unitarian Chapel* in St. Saviourgate, built in 1692. Though later altered, it preserves its original and unusual cruciform plan with a central tower-like structure. The Society of Friends began to meet in York in the late 17th century and erected a new *Meeting House* in 1817, designed by the local architects Watson and Pritchett. This was fully described in a contemporary publication, and had a galleried interior heated by warm air conveyed in ducts in the floor, a notable technical innovation. J. P. Pritchett was a prolific architect of nonconformist chapels and in 1839 designed *Salem Chapel* for the Congregationalists; the elevation with two Ionic columns *in antis* was a dominant terminal feature at the end of St. Saviourgate until it was demolished in 1963. A late work by the same architect is *Ebenezer Primitive Methodist Chapel* in Little Stonegate, now a printing works. Like many other chapels of this period, the main floor is raised above ground level to provide for a schoolroom in the basement. The Leeds architect James Simpson was responsible for *Centenary Chapel* built in St. Saviourgate in 1840 for the Wesleyan Methodists and still in use; the front has a grandiose Ionic portico with pediment, a feature not seen to best advantage in this narrow street.

MAJOR MEDIEVAL BUILDINGS

In an important medieval city such as York there were, in addition to the churches and ordinary houses, a number of larger buildings belonging essentially to an urban context and serving some sort of institutional purpose. Of the monastic houses at York only those of three orders of Friars stood within the central area and apart from short lengths of precinct wall there are no standing remains, a fate shared by Friars' houses in many other cities.

Similar in function to monastic houses, in that they provided accommodation for communal living, were three colleges connected with the Minster. The buildings of one of these, St. Sepulchre's, have long since disappeared. The outstanding survival is *St. William's College*, built for chantry priests of the Minster who lived as a community consisting of a provost and twenty-three fellows. The building was started about 1465 on a lavish scale and consists of four ranges around a courtyard, each constructed in a similar manner with a timber-framed upper floor standing on a stone-walled ground storey. After the dissolution of the College in 1546 the building was used as a private residence and by the late 19th century had been divided into a series of tenements and shops. In the early part of the present century it became the meeting place of the Convocation of the Province of York and for this purpose was extensively restored, some parts being greatly altered by the creation of large halls on the upper floors. Little of the original disposition of the rooms can now be recognised. **80** There was a short hall in the west range, raised over a cellar and extending through two storeys, and in the same range were also a kitchen and chapel. A series of doorways around the courtyard suggests that the rest of the building was planned rather like a college at Oxford or Cambridge with several staircases providing access to small rooms. Even though so little of the original plan can be determined, the College is a remarkable survival of a building occupied by a medieval institution. It also provides a closely-dated example of medieval carpentry, though with its wealth of moulded timber it stands apart from the York tradition.

The third of these establishments was the *Bedern*, which occupied a site on the east side of Goodramgate. Founded in 1252, it was a college of thirty-six Vicars Choral. Though not formally dissolved until 1936, any sense of communal life had disappeared long before, the vicars having ceased to dine in common in 1574. The architectural form of the Bedern was much less compact than St. William's College. It had a fairly dispersed layout and remains of only the two most important buildings survive, though the plans of others were revealed during recent excavations by the York Archaeological Trust. The relatively small Chapel was consecrated in the middle of the 14th century though **20** it incorporates some masonry from the previous chapel built 100 years earlier. The structure being unsafe, the roof and upper parts of the walls were removed in 1961. The Hall, a little to the east of **65** the chapel, is of about the same size and was also built in the 14th century. It, too, suffered much from alteration and dereliction in later centuries, but the splendid roof structure with scissor bracing remains largely intact. It is a unique example in the city of a stone-built open hall and has recently been restored.

The principal medieval hospital in York and one of the greatest in England was *St. Leonard's*. It occupied a site in the west corner of the Roman fortress and therefore immediately inside the city wall where it was protected externally by St. Mary's Abbey. Though traditionally founded about 937 by King Athelstan, the land where the existing remains stand was granted by William II in the late 11th century. At that time the hospital was known as St. Peter's and the later name was not generally used until the 13th century. Little is known about the buildings of the hospital and those that survive lie near or against the boundaries of the large site. The principal surviving part is a ruined 13th-century building in Museum Street which appears to be a fragment of a large first-floor infirmary **90** hall above a vaulted undercroft, with a chapel projecting at right angles. It also incorporates a vaulted **91** passage which was the entrance to the hospital from a gatehouse further to the south-west facing the River Ouse. After the dissolution in the 16th century the site of the hospital remained largely intact until St. Leonard's Place with its terrace of houses was made across it in 1835. **154**

The *Guildhall* stands on the bank of the River Ouse and is approached from St. Helen's Square **68, 69** by an arched carriageway passing through the Mansion House. The main hall itself was built between **93** 1449 and 1459, the cost of building being shared by the Corporation and the Guild of St. Christopher. It is a substantial aisled building with walls of magnesian limestone, and is lit by traceried windows all round. The low-pitched roof is carried on two rows of massive oak columns. From the time it **69** was built the hall has been the scene for civic functions of all kinds, for plays and for law courts. In 1942 it was hit by a bomb and burned out. In its present form it is a reconstruction completed in 1960; the whole of the roof and other timberwork and much of the stone of the upper parts of the walls are new.

A lower building at the river end, rising sheer from the water, contains the inner chamber, now a committee room. This is also of the middle of the 15th century and, fortunately escaping the fire of **199** 1942, retains its original roof with many carved bosses representing animal and human heads, shields-of-arms and foliage. Beneath the north aisle of the hall is Common Hall Lane, an enclosed passageway following the natural slope of the land and originally providing a direct access from St. Helen's Square to a narrow staith on the river bank. At the lower end is an impressive series of **68, 69** double-chamfered arches. The picturesque limestone buildings in Gothic style clustered around the low-pitched gable of the hall itself, best seen from across the river, are mostly of 19th-century date.

70–73 The *Merchant Adventurers' Hall*, occupying a site close to the bank of the River Foss between Fossgate and Piccadilly, is a medieval survival of the highest importance. It was built from 1357 to 1361 for the Guild of Our Lord Jesus Christ and the Blessed Virgin Mary. Though this was, at least in name, a religious guild, the mercers of York were prominent in it from the beginning and in 1430 a new charter was obtained which changed it more specifically into a merchants' company. The Hall was built on the grandest scale and consisted of two principal parts. The lower storey or **73** undercroft was used as a hospital. Its spacious interior was divided into two aisles by a row of massive oak posts with four-way bracing supporting the floor of the great hall above. The walls are built of the earliest surviving bricks in York, bought from the Carmelite Friars in 1358. At the south-east end of the undercroft is a chapel entered through a wide archway containing a late medieval timber **72** screen. The chapel was rebuilt in the 15th century and the present fittings, with two tiers of seating along each side wall disposed like a college chapel, were installed in the late 17th century. The upper **73** storey, containing the great hall, is entirely timber-framed and like the undercroft is divided into two aisles by a central row of posts. This division is expressed externally by twin gables at each end. **71** On the north-east side an addition, with a row of three timber gables, was probably built in the early 17th century. From about the 16th century onwards the interiors of both great hall and undercroft (which was still in use as a hospital until the late 19th century) were gradually divided up by inserted partitions and plaster ceilings. During an extended period of restoration in the 20th century all these accretions were cleared away revealing once again the complete timber structure.

74 The *Merchant Taylors' Hall* in Aldwark is more modest. The Taylors' Company, in its origins, was also associated with a religious guild, the Fraternity of St. John the Baptist. The hall seems to **188** have been built about 1400 as a sizeable open hall floored at ground level, with a screens passage at the north-west end. It was timber-framed but in later times, especially during the 18th century, the external walls were almost entirely rebuilt in brick. The roof structure was altered, perhaps in the later 16th century, when tie-beams were introduced to provide a stability that the original arch-braced trusses must have lacked. As in so many other medieval buildings, plaster ceilings were later introduced and the present internal appearance with the timbered roof once again exposed to view is the result of a modern restoration. Projecting to the south is a smaller hall, also originally timber-framed and, like the great hall, refaced in brick in the 18th century. A hospital, mentioned in late medieval times, was rebuilt in 1730 as a detached single-storey building to accommodate four poor **182** persons, as recorded on a stone tablet on its front wall.

75 *St. Anthony's Hall* at the corner of Aldwark and Peasholme Green is of a similar architectural concept to the Merchant Adventurers' Hall. Of the two storeys, the lower has stone-built walls and originally housed a hospital and chapel. The first floor was timber-framed and contained a great hall with aisles. The outer walls were wholly rebuilt in brick in the 17th century and inside the hall the timber arcades have been infilled with partitions to provide a series of smaller rooms in the aisles. The Hall was built in the middle of the 15th century for the Guild of St. Martin on the site of an earlier chapel of St. Anthony. The guild survived until it was dissolved in 1627 and the building was thereafter variously used as an arsenal, military hospital and prison until a bluecoat school was established in it in 1705. The school remained there right through the 19th century during which time a number of extensions were erected for it around a courtyard on the north-west side. The building is now the home of the Borthwick Institute of Historical Research.

TIMBER-FRAMED HOUSES

Though there are some slight remains of stone-built houses, of which the most important are the ruined walls of the late 12th-century Norman House in Stonegate, timber-framing was the normal **89** method of constructing town houses in the medieval period and continued in York until its use was forbidden by the City Council in 1645. Even well into the 18th century the central streets must have been mainly lined with framed buildings and the brick facade would have been a comparative rarity. Timber buildings survive in greatest number in Petergate, Stonegate, Goodramgate and **125** the Shambles. There are still a few in Coney Street, which has been developed as one of York's **124, 119** principal shopping streets, but many in Jubbergate and Pavement were lost when Parliament Street and Piccadilly were created by extensive demolitions in the 19th and early 20th centuries. When Cave sketched Fossgate about 1800 the street was still mostly formed of timber-framed houses but **3** only two or three are now left; the most recent to disappear was the former Queen's Head Inn. The **120** timber-framed houses which lined Low Ousegate, also picturesquely illustrated by Cave, were demolished for street widening when Ouse Bridge was rebuilt in 1810–20. Very few timber buildings survive in Walmgate even though the whole length of the street was built-up in 1610, according to Speed's map.

The earliest surviving timber-framed houses in the city date from the early 14th century. They include two very interesting examples of long ranges built on the edges of churchyards, the rents collected from them being used to endow chantries in the churches. Lady Row, 60–72 Goodramgate, **117** licensed in 1316, originally contained nine or ten houses, each consisting of one room about 10 by 15 feet on each of the two floors. Though much altered it remains a building of great historical importance. A similar row on the churchyard of St. Sampson's, fronting Newgate, was built about **135** 1337 but is less well preserved.

These houses exemplify one of the characteristics of timber-framed buildings: on plan they tend to be long and narrow. The earlier buildings were often sited with their longer sides parallel to the street, having lengthy frontages, but were only one room in depth. In the later medieval period it became more common for the houses to be aligned at right-angles to the street, thus presenting narrow gabled front elevations. These houses often extended backwards 30 feet or more, utilising their sites in greater depth. Where a wider frontage was available such houses were built in pairs presenting twin gables to the street like 37, 38 Shambles, and occasionally in groups of three as at **124** 16–22 Coney Street. **119**

Before the 15th century most houses were two-storeyed but thereafter three-storeyed ones became **122, 123,** very common in the main streets of the city such as Petergate or Goodramgate. Some houses built **125** with two storeys were later heightened by an additional storey; at 17, 19 Stonegate, for example, the **121** multi-gabled third storey was added in the late 16th century to a 15th-century two-storeyed range.

All timber-framed buildings in York are jettied over the street, that is, the upper storeys project beyond the ones beneath them. This is a common feature of town houses elsewhere in England. Very few houses in York are also jettied at the back, suggesting that the jettying of upper storeys was very much a matter of display. One of the few buildings jettied to both front and rear is in **122** Patrick Pool, built in the late 16th century on the churchyard of St. Sampson's.

In the central area fifteen buildings are known which originally contained open halls or rooms of similar character. It is not certain that they were all domestic halls; one of the more doubtful is an **128** irregularly-shaped three-bay range at 45 Goodramgate, of plain construction and possibly built for commercial use. The halls are mostly of two bays and occupy diverse positions in relation both to the street pattern and to other buildings with which they are connected. They are usually sited **118** behind multi-storey ranges and are very rarely on the street frontage. An exception is 111 Walmgate where a short hall only one bay in length presents an unjettied front to the street and is attached to **129** a two-storeyed range at right-angles; the hall was later divided by an inserted floor. The more characteristic position of a hall is at right-angles behind a range aligned along the street frontage. **123** 49, 51 Goodramgate is a good example. The front range is three-storeyed, and the range behind has a central open hall lit by tall windows and flanked by two-storeyed bays. The house is a northern outlier of the 'Wealden' type with an oversailing wall-plate in front of the hall.

Several first-floor halls have been recorded in York, all attributed to the late 14th or 15th centuries. **118** At the Red Lion in Merchantgate the hall, preserved only in fragmentary condition, lies parallel to Walmgate but set back about 50 feet behind a former yard. A lower two-storey range was built **130** against it in the 17th century. Other examples are 28–32 Coppergate and 35 Shambles.

In all the medieval houses in the city the top storey was originally unceiled and open to the roof **131** structure, as in the restored example at 45 Goodramgate. Usually a ceiling was later inserted to provide a greater degree of comfort, and sometimes this was boarded over to create a usable attic, **131** as at 31 Stonegate. The exact date of the introduction of attics as integral features of new buildings **121** is uncertain but the practice had become established when 12, 14 Pavement was built in the early 17th century.

In the medieval period it was normal for the timber framework to be visible both externally and internally. The interstices between the timbers were filled with stone or brick and covered with **127** plaster. Stone rubble was used for this purpose in some of the earliest buildings, as at Lady Row, Goodramgate, but the infilling was usually of thin bricks set on edge. In later centuries it became common to apply another plaster coat to existing buildings covering all the timbers as well as the previously plastered infill. By the 19th century most framed buildings in York had been so treated. **125** Some houses, notably a large group on the south-west side of Low Petergate, still present this appearance, but in the 20th century extensive restoration work on others has included removal of **121** external plaster and replacement of inserted Georgian sashes by leaded lights. Examples are 12–14 **122, 126** Pavement, 41–45 Goodramgate and the Black Swan, Peasholme Green, where later additions have received imitation framed decoration. In many interiors inserted partitions, ceilings and wallpaper **129** have been removed to reveal the full extent of the framing, as at 111 Walmgate.

The patterns of framing, in particular spacing of vertical studs and use of bracing, are a guide to **117** dating. The White Rose Cafe in Jubbergate comprises two buildings of quite different dates. The 14th-century part, to the left when seen from the south-west, has widely-spaced studs and downward bracing from the posts which mark the bays; the 17th-century part to the right has distinctly greater floor heights, closely-spaced studs and an absence of diagonal bracing.

Wall bracing is one of the most distinctive features of timber-framed construction. In York, braces generally rise upwards from vertical posts to connect with horizontal members such as middle rails and wall-plates. In jettied walls, however, they are placed in the opposite direction, as seen very clearly at 111 Walmgate. Throughout the main period of timber-framed construction, including the whole of the 15th century, braces were fairly broad with a distinct curvature, but for a short time in the later 16th century ogee-shaped braces of rather slighter scantling were fashionable. They can be seen in the third storey added to 17, 19 Stonegate and in the later part of 77 Walmgate. In the first half of the 17th century, braces were less commonly used; where they do occur, as at 30, 32 Goodramgate and 12, 14 Pavement, they are straight and much thinner than previously. **118** **121, 126** **119** **121**

The method of construction of roof trusses is also a useful guide to dating. One early form has a secondary pair of timbers, known as passing braces, parallel to the common rafters. A very good example of this was at a building, now demolished, behind 24 Coney Street, and there are fragments of another of early 14th-century date at 2 Minster Court. Almost all roof trusses erected from the early 14th to the early 16th century have a crown-post, which is an upright timber post standing centrally on the tie-beam and rising not to the apex of the roof but to a collar about two-thirds of the way up. Below the collar and supported by the crown-post is a collar-purlin, a longitudinal member to provide stiffness to the whole structure. A simple form of unbraced crown-post is at 7 Shambles, but it normally has curved braces to the tie-beam as at 37, 38 Shambles or the gabled cross-wing at 77 Walmgate. These braces are frequently crossed by a second pair connecting the tie-beam with the rafters and supporting side-purlins as at 35 Stonegate and 44 Fossgate. In these 15th-century examples the braces downwards to the tie-beam are housed into the crown-post near its head, which is itself enlarged so that it can embrace the collar-purlin and be tenoned into the collar above. In the earliest examples surviving, such as 64 Goodramgate, 15 Newgate and 45 Walmgate, the tall and slender crown-post has no enlarged head and the braces meet it much lower down. **127** **134** **130** **124** **126** **131, 133** **127, 135**

The crown-post is common in south-eastern England in the later medieval period but does not occur widely in the north. In York it seems to have been discontinued about the early 16th century and was succeeded for a time by a form of truss with substantial principal rafters immediately below the common rafters, extending only from the tie-beam to the collar. An early example is the central truss in a former open hall at 2 Coffee Yard. **132**

THE TREASURER'S HOUSE

The largest single house in central York, and totally exceptional, is the Treasurer's House situated to the north-east of the Minster and now a National Trust property. The complex includes extensive parts to the rear now known as Gray's Court. The house was originally the dwelling of the Treasurer of the Minster, whose office was very richly endowed. Of the medieval house there is one late 12th-century wall still *in situ* within Gray's Court, with a round-arched window. The main body of the Treasurer's House facing south-west over the Dean's Park was built in the 16th and 17th centuries after the abolition of the office of Treasurer. It was probably begun by George Young, son of Archbishop Young (1561-8), but there seems to have been a major reconstruction by George's grandson Thomas who occupied the property in the period 1628-48. It must have been he who provided a new frontispiece with superimposed orders to the central entrance on the south-west side and **81-88** **183** **82** **83**

88 extended and refaced the gabled wings which project forward. He also probably built a new gallery on the north-east side, standing over a colonnade formed of reset 12th-century columns, now forming the core of Gray's Court. From the late 17th until the end of the 19th century the house passed through a succession of owners, many of whom made alterations or small additions, and was gradually divided up into a number of small tenements. The process of consolidation began in the late 19th century when Mr. Frank Green of York bought the parts which now constitute the Treasurer's House and reunited them, making considerable alterations to the central range where a

81 new large hall rising through two storeys was created. Shortly afterwards, Edwin Gray who occupied Gray's Court undertook a similar operation of restoration combined with quite extensive alterations.

PUBLIC BUILDINGS OF THE 18TH AND 19TH CENTURIES

In a city like York that was an administrative and judicial centre and a focus of social life in the county, there are a number of buildings which were erected to provide appropriate settings for a range of communal and official functions, and which stand out from the many private houses lining the streets either because of size or of architectural singularity or pretension. Some buildings of this type in the city are of such a size that when they were erected in the 18th and 19th centuries there was very little space available in the crowded central area to provide sites large enough for them. They consequently lie outside the geographical limits of this book. Educational institutions such as the Diocesan Training College and St. Peter's School, hospitals like Bootham Park and The Retreat, the workhouse in Huntington Road and the Cavalry Barracks in Fulford Road all had to be built well outside the city walls.

93–95 The *Mansion House*, the official residence of the Lord Mayor, is the foremost civic building in York. Facing St. Helen's Square, it conceals behind it the Guildhall and the late-Victorian Council Chamber and offices which are reached by a carriageway passing through the lower storey. It was built between 1726 and 1733 for the purpose it still serves; the frequent attribution of the design to Lord Burlington is without foundation and unlikely. The front elevation, rising high above its

93 neighbours, betrays perhaps the influence of the 17th-century Queen's Gallery at Somerset House in London with its giant order standing on an arched and rusticated basement; the crowning pediment which also forms part of the Mansion House design incorporates the city's coat-of-arms.

The internal planning is generally similar to other large Georgian houses in York but is different in one respect. At the front the two upper floors are united into a single magnificent chamber, the

95 State Room, extending across the whole frontage, 50 feet long and 28 feet wide with panelled walls articulated by pilasters, a coved ceiling and a fireplace at each end. In one of the smaller rooms

179 behind is a white marble chimney-piece, believed to have been brought from the Adam brothers' Adelphi Buildings in London.

The Mansion House contains the York Civic Plate and Insignia. The earliest and most outstanding

64 item is the sword of the Emperor Sigismund which originally hung over his stall as a Knight of the Garter in St. George's Chapel, Windsor. In 1439, two years after his death, it was given to the city, a benefaction recorded by an inscription on the sword itself. Other items illustrated are a silver centre-piece of 1796 with a figure of Justice under a domed canopy, a gold cup of 1671, a silver-gilt cup of

92 1679 bearing the city arms, and the Great Mace, also silver-gilt, made in 1647.

96–99 The *Assembly Rooms* in Blake Street symbolise the city's position as the social capital of Yorkshire in the early-Georgian period. They are an authentic work by the 3rd Earl of Burlington, an amateur architect and apostle of Palladianism in England whose own country seat was at Londesbrough in the East Riding. The principal feature in this pioneer neo-Classical building is the Great Assembly Room, to which everything else is subordinate. This celebrated room, 100 feet long, is based directly **98** on the 'Egyptian Hall' which the 16th-century Italian architect Andrea Palladio published in his *Four Books of Architecture* in 1570. The unique character of the room derives from a peristyle of closely-spaced Corinthian columns supporting a tall clerestorey which provides the entire natural lighting. The plan also provides for a Lesser Assembly Room on the north side and a series of smaller rooms **97, 99** which retain a number of original fittings. The street front was completely altered in 1828 when the **96** York architect J. P. Pritchett refaced it in stone and added an Ionic portico.

The *De Grey Rooms* in St. Leonard's Place, built by subscription in 1841–2, were designed by **100** another local architect, G. T. Andrews. The impetus for the erection of this building was given by the Earl de Grey and officers of the Yorkshire Hussars who required suitable accommodation for their annual mess. It was also intended to provide a venue for other events and meetings for which the Assembly Rooms were not suitable, a purpose it still serves admirably. At one end of the elegant cement-rendered elevation with its tall windows and iron balconies is De Grey House, slightly earlier in date than the Rooms and the only house to be built of a projected terrace.

Foss Bridge, which spans the lesser of the two rivers at York, was built in 1811 to the designs of **116** Peter Atkinson junior who was at the same time also engaged in rebuilding the much larger three-arched Ouse Bridge (not illustrated in this book). It replaced a bridge which was largely or entirely of the 15th century and which was itself on the site of earlier bridges that formed the only link with the Walmgate area of the city.

Immediately beside the bridge is *Dorothy Wilson's Hospital*, one of only two almshouses remaining **153** in the central area. Established under the will of the lady whose name it commemorates, the hospital was at first accommodated in her own house on the site. This was rebuilt in 1765 and again in 1812 following the rebuilding of Foss Bridge, the dates being recorded on inscribed stone tablets in the **182** front wall, one of which was reset from the previous building. The hospital is built in a compact house-like shape with a single front door to the street and internal corridor access to each room; this characteristically urban form is found elsewhere in York at Wandesford Hospital, Bootham and Middleton's Hospital, Skeldergate.

Lady Hewley's Hospital in St. Saviourgate has a more spread-out plan commonly found in rural establishments of this kind. A long stone-faced range in Tudor style has a series of doorways giving access to the individual dwellings. The warden's house is a separate block, double-fronted but with **152** the gable-end to the street and in the same style as the almshouses. In the end wall is a reset inscribed tablet with sculptured arms of the foundress, brought from the original building in Tanner Row. **182** The existing buildings date from 1840.

J. P. Pritchett, the architect of Lady Hewley's Hospital, did much work for the Dean and Chapter. With his partner Charles Watson he designed the building in Minster Yard to the south of the Minster which is now the *Song School*. This was built in 1830–33, on part of the garden of the then **150** recently-demolished Old Deanery, for St. Peter's School which moved in 1844 to larger premises at Clifton. The original plan as shown in the architects' drawings comprised little more than three large schoolrooms, now divided up by inserted floors and partitions to provide smaller classrooms.

On an adjoining site and also designed by Pritchett is another stone-faced building in Tudor style, now *8 and 9 Minster Yard*. This was designed in 1837 as a Wills Office for the Dean and Chapter, but **151**

195 was completed as a pair of houses. The style is reflected in the interior fittings, such as the staircases with cast-iron balusters, and clearly it was felt at that time that such a late medieval appearance was appropriate for the Minster Close. One of the houses is directly connected to buildings in Low

6 Petergate (now Nos. 48 and 50), which are in plain late-Georgian style even though built as part of the same project as the Minster Yard houses.

A new class of building to appear in the city centre in the second quarter of the 19th century was

153 the bank. The earliest is the *York Savings Bank* at the corner of St. Helen's Square and Blake Street, built in 1829–30 also to the designs of Watson and Pritchett. The rounded corner enables the two adjacent elevations to form a single composition in a refined classical style, the first floor articulated by engaged monolithic columns and pilasters of the Corinthian order. The doorway on the corner is not original but a later alteration very carefully executed, and in 1924 an extension, matching in style the original facade, was built in Blake Street. The first floor of the original building consisted

155 of little more than a large and impressive boardroom. The *Midland Bank* in Parliament Street was built in 1835 for the York City and County Bank and was an original part of the scheme for this new market place. The architects were P. F. Robinson and G. T. Andrews; the latter, who did much prominent work in York, was also responsible for the head office of the Yorkshire Insurance Company

155 in St. Helen's Square. Stone-faced in the best ashlar, the design is based ultimately on Sangallo's *Palazzo Farnese* in Rome though more immediately on Sir Charles Barry's club buildings, particularly the Athenaeum in Manchester. The name of the company and the date of its foundation (1823) are inscribed boldly in the frieze.

156 The *Midland Bank* in Nessgate was built in 1839 for the Yorkshire Agricultural and Commercial Bank which had to close in 1842 because of expenditure on 'injudiciously building elaborate and expensive premises at York and Whitby'. The main part of the building, standing at the corner of High Ousegate, bears this out for both street elevations are richly furnished with rusticated masonry, balustrades and pedimented windows though the adjacent manager's house has a simple brick front. The architects were the brothers J. B. and W. Atkinson who did more work in York in the middle part of the 19th century than any other firm. Another special-purpose building by them is the

156 *Masonic Hall* in St. Saviourgate, built in 1845–6 for the Institute of Popular Science and Literature; it originally had a lecture hall, news and reading rooms, library and classrooms but has been much altered inside.

HOUSES FROM 1650 TO 1850

In the middle of the 17th century the use of timber-framing ceased and a new kind of house appeared in the city streets which presented a completely different appearance from the gabled houses with projecting upper floors which had been normal in earlier centuries. A distinctive style gradually developed characterised by the use of brick as a building material even though occasionally cement rendered, by windows of vertical proportion usually fitted with hung sashes and by classical detailing used for such features as doorways and eaves cornices.

The advent of brick as the normal building material for small houses in York can be pinpointed exactly to January 1645 when the City Council prohibited the use of timber-framing. There are only

184, 185 a few houses surviving from the later part of the 17th century, but from about 1700 onwards there was extensive and continual rebuilding on city-centre plots where timber-framed houses must formerly have stood. Those who could not afford to rebuild completely compromised by replacing former jettied fronts with brick walls built upright from the ground and by refitting interiors to such an extent that original framing was entirely hidden from view.

Nearly all the largest town houses in the central area date from before 1760. They were mostly built for leading citizens, especially those who had achieved the coveted office of Lord Mayor, or as town houses for the county aristocracy and gentry. They were normally planned with three reception rooms on the ground floor and a substantial saloon on the first, the kitchen being either at the back of the ground floor or in the basement. One characteristic feature is the presence of two staircases. The broad and spacious main stair is usually at the back of the house but directly visible from the front door and rises only to the first floor, while the secondary one placed to the side is much more tightly planned and serves all the floors. Externally they have the characteristic double-fronted appearance with a central doorway.

The most outstanding of the group is *Fairfax House* in Castlegate. This was built for Charles, **101–108**
Viscount Fairfax of Emley, to the designs of John Carr, the most celebrated architect who worked in York. It seems to have been started in the early 1750s, but fitting out of the interior was not completed until 1762 or later. The pedimented front elevation is rather crowded and many of the **101**
stone dressings appear to have been cut back flush with the brick face. The glory of the house lies in the interior, especially the plasterwork. Two rooms on each of the ground and first floors have very elaborate ceilings and the stair-hall is similarly treated. The staircase balustrade is distinctive in being **108**
made of iron by the York smith Maurice Tobin.

Almost directly across the street is *Castlegate House*, built in 1762–3 for Peter Johnson, Recorder of **109–111**
York, also to the designs of John Carr. Standing detached and set back some way from the street behind a forecourt, the distinguishing feature of the front is the row of first-floor windows set within arched recesses. At the rear are a pair of canted bay windows, a favourite feature of Carr; between them, lighting the staircase, is a Venetian window under a wider arch, another motif typical of the architect. Unlike Fairfax House, the fittings in Castlegate House are relatively restrained.

Peasholme House is of similar size though it is rather less refined in execution. It was built in 1752 **112**
as a speculation by a carpenter, Robert Heworth, and was the subject of a remarkable rescue in the mid-1970s when a warehouse that had stood in front of it for nearly 100 years was removed and the house thoroughly renovated.

The *Judge's Lodging*, Lendal, is a prominent and distinctive house stylistically rather apart from the **113–115**
main stream of 18th-century York houses. Built for Dr. Clifton Wintringham in the second or third decade of the 18th century it became the Judge's Lodging in 1806, a function it served until recently. The house is tall, with a basement at very little below the present ground level. A double-branched flight of steps ascends to the main floor where the entrance is, unusually, in a Venetian opening; behind it is a square entrance hall with engaged columns around the walls. The staircase, placed to one side of the house, is shut off from the hall by a door and not visually connected with it in the usual manner. The stair is exceptional in the city in rising in a single elliptical flight, leading to a **114, 115**
central vaulted passage on the first floor. The principal rooms do not face the street but are at the rear overlooking a small garden. In several respects this house betrays the hand of an architect whose work does not appear elsewhere in York.

Other houses of this type are the *Red House*, Duncombe Place, built on part of the site of the **139**
former St. Leonard's Hospital in the early part of the century for Sir William Robinson, Lord Mayor of the city in 1700, and the *Old Residence* in Minster Yard, now detached though formerly but one of **139**

140   a row of houses in a street which bounded the east and south sides of the Minster choir. At 26 St. Saviourgate the regularity of the front elevation is disrupted at the left-hand side by a second door-

140   way, to a side-passage leading through to the otherwise inaccessible rear garden. 62 Low Petergate is one of the most distinctive houses of this type with tall windows on both storeys and a crowning Doric entablature across the entire front. The house, built about 1725 by John Shaw, Proctor of the Court at York, on part of the site of the former Talbot Inn, has service wings to each side which were much enlarged in the later 19th century. Two houses of the same general type, from different

144   ends of the century, have overall pediment-like gables: at Cromwell House, Ogleforth, the gable

143   has been rebuilt in modern times; 20 St. Andrewgate has characteristics associated with the York architect Thomas Atkinson who lived in the street and this may have been his own house, designed by himself.

138   A few houses of substantial size have less regular plans. *Cumberland House*, built by William Cornwall, a tanner and brewer who was twice Lord Mayor, is prominently situated on the King's Staith overlooking the river. The stone-walled and vaulted basement entered direct from the staith is subject to regular flooding and the entrance to the house, instead of being in the usual central position, is in the side wall at almost the highest possible level in the sharply rising street to the right,

138   well above flood level. *Oliver Sheldon House*, Aldwark, has one of the longest street fronts of any house in York, but the irregular planning is due to the complicated historical development of the house. The early Georgian brick elevation was added by Charles Redman, also twice Lord Mayor, to an earlier structure.

Pairs or larger groups of houses built as a single operation recur throughout the 18th century. An interesting redevelopment was in High Ousegate where a disastrous fire in 1694 destroyed thirty houses on the north-west side of the street. Most of these were probably small and timber-framed, and some would have been facing alleys leading back from the street. On the street frontage of 160

144   feet three pairs of houses were erected in the early part of the 18th century. Nos. 11 and 12, the largest houses, were built by Samuel Buxton, a grocer who had been Sheriff of the city in 1696. As designed, there was a central passage on the ground floor, perhaps on the site of an ancient alley, from which both houses were entered. Though the elevation is symmetrical, with giant pilasters flanking the central bay and at the ends, the plans of the houses are dissimilar and they do not appear

144   to have been built in a single campaign. The two houses of the second pair, Nos. 13 and 14, of more modest size, were similarly both entered from a central passageway with a round archway towards the street. Of the third pair only one half survives, refaced in late-Victorian brickwork.

Larger groups of houses forming short terraces are not a common characteristic of Georgian York.

137   An early instance is 2–4 Precentor's Court, a range built by the Dean and Chapter near the beginning of the 18th century. There are four houses in the group but Nos. 4 and 4a are both entered from the same passage with a single front door to the street. These, each with a single room at the front lit by two windows, and a smaller room and a staircase to the rear, are particularly well preserved.

Two outstanding terraces of houses dating from a little before the middle of the 18th century are

4   16–22 St. Saviourgate and 3–9 New Street. At St. Saviourgate there are four houses in the row and a fifth front door at the extreme right-hand side is for a passage that leads directly through to the rear. The houses are not identical inside and the two central ones were built with interlocking L-shaped plans so that one of the two front rooms of No. 20 is directly in front of one of the rear rooms of No. 18. Cumberland Row in New Street is so named, according to tradition, because it

was being roofed on the day that the Duke of Cumberland passed through York in 1746 after the battle of Culloden. It was built by Charles Mitley, a carver, and his brother-in-law William Carr, a carpenter and joiner; there were originally six houses in the terrace but two have been demolished and replaced by replicas. Each has three windows towards the street and the common town-house plan of, on each floor, a single room at the front, another at the rear and the staircase in between, top-lit from a roof-light. The houses are well fitted out and there are a number of notable chimney-pieces. **176**

The building of terraces of this length was a rare event in 18th-century York because the requisite amount of land with a street frontage of sufficient length did not often become available in the already densely built-up central area. Cumberland Row was built in a street which had been only newly-formed at that time. Several blocks of three houses were built in this period. One is 33, 35 **149** St. Saviourgate and 10 Spen Lane. As it stands at a street corner the end house is entered in the gable wall thus eliminating the space-consuming entrance passage that the other two houses have alongside the front rooms. This group of houses has been much altered by conversion to flats. Another block of three is 15–21 Blake Street which is four-storeyed and was built in 1773 by Thomas Haxby, a **143** musical instrument maker who lived in one of the houses himself. The occasion for rebuilding these properties was a widening of the street. Adjacent houses were rebuilt soon afterwards. One of these is No. 25, at the corner of Stonegate; the long elevation to Blake Street gives a deceptive appearance **143** of the size of the house and it is in fact less than seven feet deep at the north-west end.

Longer terraces of houses were a more common feature in the early 19th century. In the densely built-up central core these were occasioned by street widenings, such as in Spurriergate in 1841, or **156** by the clearance of old buildings as in the formation of Parliament Street in 1835. The only example of the archetypal Regency or early-Victorian stuccoed terrace development, so common in London and south coastal towns, is St. Leonard's Place. Built from 1834 onwards to the designs of John **154** Harper, its curved elevation faced a new street driven through the site of the medieval St. Leonard's Hospital. In addition to seven houses, it contained a library and premises for the Yorkshire Club. Behind the uniform front the internal arrangements were left to individual leaseholders. On expiry of the 99-year leases the terrace reverted to York Corporation which now uses it as council offices. Another example of a row of houses built on a fan-shaped plan is 24–36 High Petergate, designed **8** in 1838 by J. P. Pritchett when the west approach to the Minster was opened up. The cheaper nature of the job is indicated by the way in which, rather than a smooth continuous curve for the front elevation, each of the small houses has a flat facade.

After the opening of the railway to York in 1841 the rate of construction of artisan housing increased. Much of this development lay outside the confines of the walled city, but in the Walmgate area space was still available for street developments such as George Street. **149**

Much Georgian house construction was of individual dwellings on sites that must previously have been occupied by timber-framed buildings. The typical smaller house has two rooms on each floor, with an entrance hall beside the front room and the staircase placed either between front and back rooms or at the rear with a window on the half-landing. One good example, on a slightly larger than average scale, is 24 St. Saviourgate. On the first floor the saloon occupied the full width of the **141** front of the house, lit by three windows, but the floor above was divided into smaller rooms for bedchambers. Other single-fronted houses of substantial size include 18 Blake Street built about 1789 **146** for Mrs. Elizabeth Woodhouse, its great height providing a strong feature in the street, and 23 High

147
196 Petergate, a refined design built 1779–80 for Robert Thornton and containing a most elegant cantilevered staircase on an elliptical plan.

147 *Melrose House* in St. Sampson's Square represents a type which has a four-bay front elevation
with the door placed in the second bay to provide a small room to one side. The distinctive appearance
of this house derives from the hipped roof which is a rare feature in the city centre. Even though it
was normal for the roof at the front of a house to be pitched, gables remained common at the rear
136 throughout the Georgian period. For a time around the beginning of the 18th century gables shaped
to various outlines were fashionable.

Though most houses were planned in depth backwards from the street, there were some exceptions.
142 14 St. Saviour's Place, built as the manse for a Wesleyan chapel which stood immediately behind it,
is more suburban in appearance. Set back behind a garden and double-fronted it is only one room
deep with but two rooms on each floor, the central window lighting the staircase. Houses standing in
142 certain positions, such as street corners, tend to have irregular plans, like 10 Minster Yard built by
148 Dean Fountayne in 1753–5. 8 Chapter House Street, formerly the rectory of Holy Trinity Church,
Goodramgate, has virtually no street frontage, its main elevation being towards the garden.

From about 1770 onwards, many houses in the main streets were four storeys high. Two of the
143, 142 earliest are 1 and 3 Feasegate and 4 High Petergate is a very good example, rising high above its
neighbours. These four-storeyed houses have low-pitched roofs which do not provide enough
space for habitable attics whereas many three-storeyed houses of the earlier period, such as 26, 28
142 Pavement, have roofs of steeper pitch containing attics lit by dormer windows. The extension of
houses upwards to four storeys was, in effect, carrying walls up around the attics to make them into
full storeys, albeit with fairly low ceiling heights.

149 In the minor streets of the city many houses are only two-storeyed. 42 St. Andrewgate is one
149 example from a little before the mid 18th century and further along the street Nos. 48, 50 form a
typical small pair of the 19th century; the arched carriageway is a later insertion, very carefully
executed.

FEATURES AND FITTINGS OF DOMESTIC BUILDINGS

Doorways

159 In the early 18th century external doorcases were usually of stone, generally with a bolection-
moulding as at 26 St. Saviourgate and Cromwell House, Ogleforth. At Cumberland House there
are also pilaster-like side-panels and a segmental pediment on spendidly carved consoles. In the later
part of the 18th century doorways normally had semicircular fanlights with radial glazing bars.
Pedimented surrounds were of timber, sometimes with applied ornaments of composition as at 23
160, 161 High Petergate. Doorcases of the early 19th century are generally not so well proportioned and less
refined than those of the late 18th. There was more often a straight cornice rather than a pediment
and fanlights were usually rectangular with narrow lights around the margins, as at 3 Monk Bar
Court. At 20 St. Andrewgate the segmental fanlight reflects the shape of the arched recess within
which the doorcase is set and at the Midland Bank, Parliament Street, is a wholly exceptional doorway
with Greek Doric columns supporting a full entablature.

162, 163 Internal doors were almost always framed, the battened door commonly used in the rural country-
side of Yorkshire being rarely found in the city centre. The framing creates a panelled effect; 4 Minster
Yard is typical of the early 18th century, with the edges of the panels covered by planted mouldings

and the smallest panel in the middle. During the greater part of the century the standard door had six panels. The door surround or architrave was moulded in all but the meanest examples; it was sometimes enriched with egg-and-dart and other motifs as at Gray's Court. At 31 Stonegate, the rich **163** composition decoration is probably by the late 18th-century owner of the house, John Staveley, a carver and gilder. In the more ambitious interiors, doorcases were frequently surmounted by an entablature with or without a pediment; Fairfax House has a number of good examples. **107**

Plasterwork

The Jacobean period of the early 17th century was one of outstanding achievement in the execution of plaster ceilings. The few examples which survive in York are not in major buildings. At 5, 7 Coney Street, houses with Georgian fronts concealing earlier work, there was a ceiling on the ground **164** floor, photographed many years ago but now either destroyed or concealed behind modern covering. It had ribs making formal geometrical patterns, softened by decorative features. Ceilings at 24 Coney **164** Street and Oliver Sheldon House are similar in spirit though based on different patterns. The first-**166** floor ceiling at 7 Coney Street is composed of a much less rigid network of scrolls and incorporates **165** birds, fruit and masks. That at 2 Minster Court is stylistically different with much broader and **166** flatter ribs.

Early 18th-century plaster ceilings over staircases at 10 Lendal, Cumberland House and Oliver **167, 168** Sheldon House, Aldwark, though differing in detailed treatment, all have a similar general plan of a large central oval between four small spandrel panels and flanked on one or both sides by rectangles. The first two have, as a border, a rather similar coving decorated with leaves, but at Aldwark there is, in a different tradition, a full cornice. The ceiling over the staircase at 62 Low Petergate, with a **168** more elaborate pattern in a restrained baroque manner, is unique in York; the central feature illustrates Aesculapius and Hygieia.

The most outstanding plaster ceilings of the middle part of the 18th century are those in Fairfax **102–106** House, Castlegate. The only plasterer whose name can be definitely associated with this house is James Henderson of York but both in quality and because of the presence of certain motifs it seems quite likely that Giuseppe Cortese, the Swiss-Italian *stuccatore* who did much work in Yorkshire and northern England at this time, may well have been primarily responsible. Work from the same hand is apparent at 1 Minster Court though on a much more limited scale. **169**

There is not very much plasterwork in the central area dating from the later phase of the 18th century when the influence of Robert Adam became dominant. The best example of the delicate but more rigidly geometrical patterns typical of the style is in the drawing room at Castlegate House. **169**

Panelling

Early 17th-century wainscotted walls are generally framed in small panels, usually five in height. Very rarely does such panelling survive untouched by later alterations. That at the Black Swan, **170** Peasholme Green, is typical in having clearly been reset, though it would almost certainly have been made for the building. Sometimes a limited amount of carved woodwork was incorporated, usually as a frieze at the top, as at 58 Stonegate, a 14th-century building where a first-floor room was wains-**170** cotted in the Jacobean period.

Wainscotting was frequently used as a wall covering during the first half of the 18th century but very little thereafter. One of the distinguishing features of this period is a moulded chair rail about

2–3 feet above floor level. Below it are small panels, with tall panels above extending up to a moulded cornice. In the early 18th century the panels project forward a little from the framing and have

172 raised bolection-mouldings round their borders; examples of these are at 39 Coney Street and 4 Precentor's Court. In more ambitious rooms, round-arched niches with display shelves flank the

171 fireplace. A good example of this is at Cumberland House. At 70 Walmgate there is an interesting room where the round-headed motif is also picked up in some of the wall panels. The latter room also has a feature, popular in York especially around the years 1710–20, of pilasters flanking the

115 fireplace; this also occurs at the Judge's Lodging. By the middle of the century panels were broader in proportion and usually either plain and sunk behind the rails and muntins which defined them, as

173 at 18 St. Saviourgate, or with moulded surrounds much more delicate than those of the early part of

173 the century. The saloon at 39 Coney Street, a very elegant and well-preserved example, typifies this. At this period the dado below the chair rail was left plain.

Fireplaces

Seventeenth-century fireplaces with their low segmental or three-centred arches were sometimes left

174 unadorned, especially when in a kitchen as at the Treasurer's House, but in principal rooms they were

175 ornamented with carved and panelled surrounds and overmantels. The best of these is at Herbert House, Pavement, though it has had some modern restoration.

In the 18th century the fireplace openings in principal rooms have surrounds in the form of a moulded architrave. In the early part of the century the profile is a bolection-moulding; one example

178 is at Cumberland House. Fine overmantels are a notable feature around the middle part of the

176 century especially in panelled rooms. At Cumberland Row, New Street, there are several, one with a sunburst in the central panel, and they are frequently surmounted by broken pediments. The sources for these features were designs in builders' pattern books which by the mid-century were appearing in increasing numbers. One of the most prolific authors of these books was Batty Langley,

177 and fireplaces with their overmantels at 19 Colliergate and 70 Walmgate can be traced to him as a source, though the proportions and small details may differ.

Ornamental decoration is often found on otherwise quite humble chimney-pieces. On one at

179 3 Stonegate there is rich carving on the frieze and the projecting central panel. Later in the century, ornament was of composition cast in moulds and is in lower relief; it is also generally applied more

180 thinly and gracefully as at 7 Minster Yard. The names of two such makers of composition ornament are known: one was Thomas Wolstenholme who lived in Gillygate, a street just outside the city

179 walls. Motifs that can certainly be ascribed to him have been identified at 39 Coney Street; exact copies of the central panel depicting Minerva have been found in several other houses in York. 31 Stonegate was owned in the late 18th century by John Staveley, a carver and gilder, and the

180 exceptionally elaborate decoration on a fireplace and other features there must surely be attributed to him.

In these later 18th-century fireplaces, the opening itself is framed by thin marble slips. Earlier, especially in the second quarter of the century, stone was popular for the whole surround. This was

180 treated fairly simply with small mouldings on the arrises, as at 9 New Street and 10 Precentor's Court, or with fielded panelling in shallow relief, as displayed at 45 Stonegate.

Windows

The earliest windows in a domestic context in York date from the 12th century. The outstanding example is at the ruined Norman House in Stonegate. Here a two-light window with a waterleaf **183** capital to the central shaft is well preserved but can only be seen from what was originally the inside of the building. At Gray's Court is a simpler round-headed window of the same period. Thirteenth and fourteenth-century single-light windows are at St. Leonard's Hospital and in the undercroft **183** walls of the Merchant Adventurers' Hall.

Very little survives of windows in timber-framed buildings since they have almost all been removed for the insertion of larger, or differently proportioned, sash windows. At 23 Stonegate, **184** there is a large window, eight lights wide, with ovolo-moulded timber mullions and transom. In the middle and later 17th century some mullioned windows, at least on back elevations, were constructed entirely in brickwork. The mullions were usually later removed to allow for sashes, but there is one good surviving example at 2 Coffee Yard where the openings have been bricked up. At the rear of **184** 38 Goodramgate is an almost unique survival in the city of a bay window of the period though, as so often elsewhere, the brick mullions have gone.

In the late 17th century moulded brickwork was used as an additional enrichment, particularly around windows. The most fanciful example was the Dutch House, Ogleforth, with its closely- **185** spaced projecting pedimented windows. Rather simpler versions of pediments in brickwork are in the rear walls at 23 and 25 Walmgate, and in much the same spirit is the upward thrust of the moulded brick string over the staircase window at 1 Coffee Yard.

Staircases

Staircases with timber balustrades do not survive in York from earlier than the middle of the 17th century though at 35 Stonegate some sturdy early 17th-century balusters have been reset into the **189** uppermost flight leading to the attic. Later 17th-century stairs all have close strings, and the more ambitious examples such as at 64 Low Petergate and the Black Swan, Peasholme Green, have robust turned balusters and square newel-posts rising to ball-finials. These early staircases ascend around square wells usually with three fairly short flights between each storey. In the early 18th century a few of the larger stairs, such as Judges' Court, still had close strings, but in the most up-to-date **190** houses the cut string was usually employed. In some stairs, such as those at Cumberland House and 10 Lendal, the string is entirely eliminated and the steps appear to be cantilevered, perhaps in imitation **191** of stone steps, though in fact they overlap each other to such an extent that raking bearers can be concealed within the timber casing.

Splat balusters, which were thin planks cut to a wavy or shaped outline, like those at 4a Precentor's **190** Court, were occasionally used around 1700 in cheap work. Throughout the 18th century, however, balusters were normally turned, with the upper part usually in the form of a classical column and generally plain as at 8 New Street but occasionally fluted as at 31 St. Saviourgate. There, exception- **190, 191** ally, the square newel-posts are also fluted. At the Judge's Lodging the oak balusters of the main **114** stair, like so much else about this house, are unique in the city; each one is a miniature Ionic column complete with voluted capitals. Twisted shafts were also occasionally used, generally as one of three standing on each step as at Cumberland House. At 62 Low Petergate there are balusters with two **191, 196** separate but entwined twisted stems. The lower part of each baluster had a variety of turned features in the earlier part of the century, as at 10 Lendal, but from about 1750 onwards this settled down to **191** a much more limited repertoire principally comprising a bulb-shape as at 9 New Street or an urn **192** feature of the kind seen at Cromwell House, Ogleforth, or 39 Coney Street. In the second half of the **193**

193 century the open string was much more commonly used with, normally, only two balusters standing on each tread; the close spacing of the balusters at 18 Blake Street is unusual so late in the century.

After the uniformity of the late 18th century, the first half of the 19th witnessed a much greater degree of invention in stair design and cast-iron balusters became more widely used after about 1830. These were mostly made at the Walmgate iron foundry of John Walker. A book of patterns produced by the firm includes several designs found in York, especially in the houses in St. Leonard's

194, 195 Place. The iron balusters at 23 Stonegate include the serpents of Aesculapius in acknowledgement of the medical profession of the owner of the house.

Carved Woodwork

Wood carving of the medieval period in York is limited to a very small number of buildings. In an

31 ecclesiastical setting, there are bosses on the ceiling of St. Cuthbert's Church which mostly represent

199 foliage though seven are of bearded or grotesque heads. In the old Inner Chamber at the Guildhall the intersections of the ceiling beams are also marked by bosses of mid 15th-century date and, as at St. Cuthbert's, several depict grotesque faces. Other subjects include the royal arms, merchants' marks and the Virgin and Child. The most outstanding carving of the 15th century is at St. William's College. On curved brackets in the coving below the jettied first floor are numerous carvings of full

198 figures. St. Christopher and the Virgin and Child are depicted to each side of the doorway in the south front and around the inner courtyard are figures representing the Labours of the Months.

197 An isolated example of mid 16th-century carving, at 62 Low Petergate, is a door made up of six carved panels brought from a house in the Bedern. They represent a school of carving otherwise

175 unknown in York. Apart from chimney-pieces such as that in the Herbert House, the limited amount of 17th-century decorative carving extant is generally on friezes in panelled rooms, of which the

170, 197 best example is at 58 Stonegate. 18th-century wood carving is concentrated on chimney-pieces and

85, 107 doorcases in the grander houses, as at the Treasurer's House and Gray's Court, and at Fairfax House. Two accomplished examples in a different setting, both dating from the same period, are the scrolled

200 monsters at the top and bottom of the staircase dados at Oliver Sheldon House and 62 Low Petergate.

181 ### Leadwork

Many lead rainwater heads and fall-pipes survive from the 18th century, but at 23 Stonegate there is a unique example dated as early as 1590, made as a plain box-shape with battlementing around the top. The characteristic earlier Georgian type has concave sides, sometimes with a centre section brought forward as at 5 High Ousegate, and though these continued until quite late in the century the rounded inverted bell-form was by then gaining in popularity. Dates and owners' initials often appear; the elephant on 52 Low Petergate was the crest of Dean Fountayne who built the house. An order by the City Council in May 1763 for the fitting of spouts to the fronts of houses is responsible for the great concentration of dated examples from that year and shortly afterwards.

Printed in England for Her Majesty's Stationery Office by Raithby, Lawrence & Company Limited at the De Montfort Press:
Leicester and London   Dd 699043 C 100

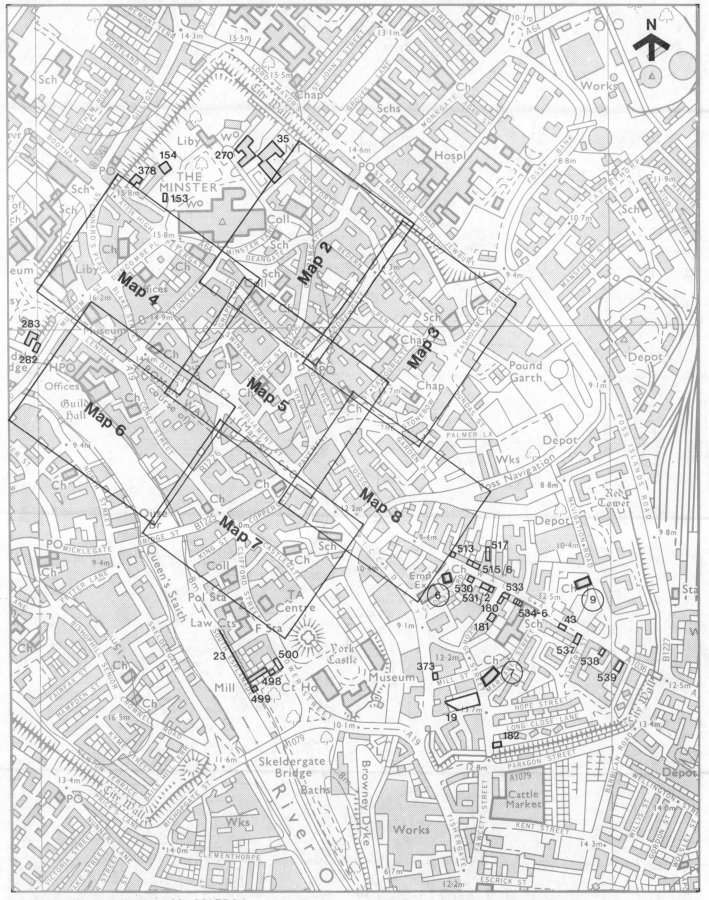

MAP 1 showing area covered by MAPS 2-8.

MAP 2. Monuments in the Goodramgate area.

Scale 1:1250

Made by Ordnance Survey, Southampton. Crown copyright reserved.

Scale 1:1250

MAP 3. Monuments in the St. Saviourgate area.

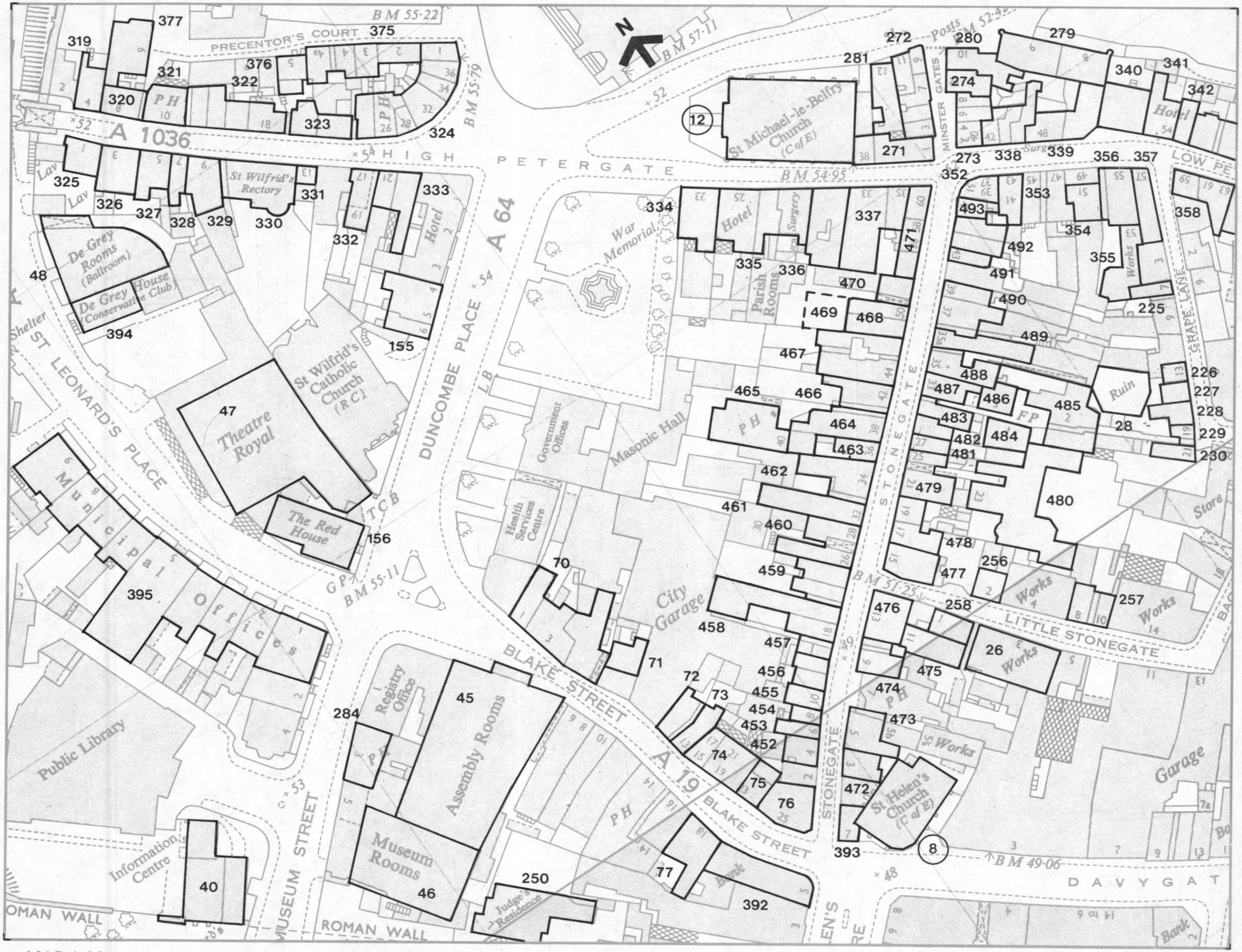

MAP 4. Monuments in the High Petergate and Stonegate area.

Scale 1:1250

Made by Ordnance Survey, Southampton. Crown copyright reserved.

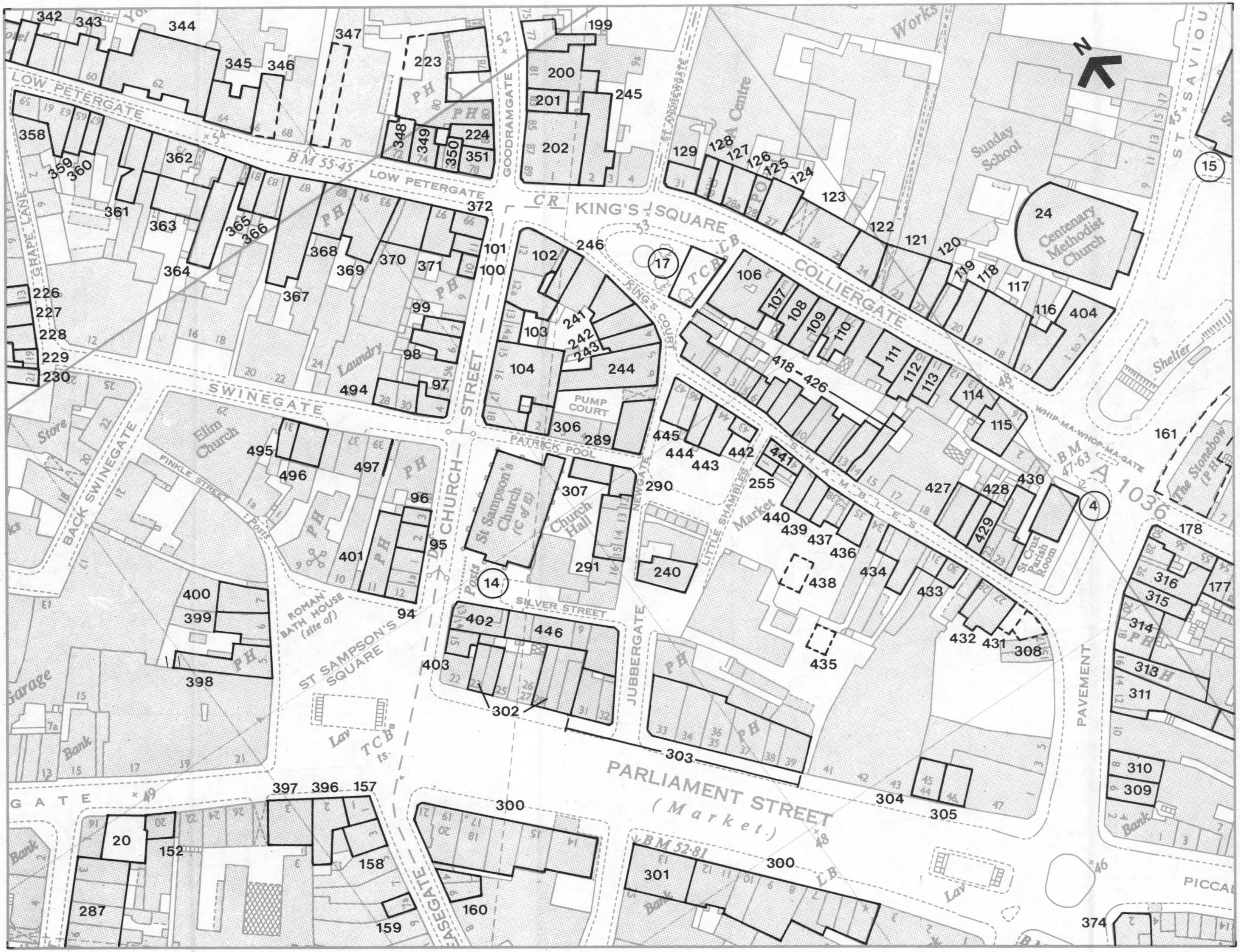

MAP 5. Monuments in the Low Petergate and Shambles area.

Scale 1:1250

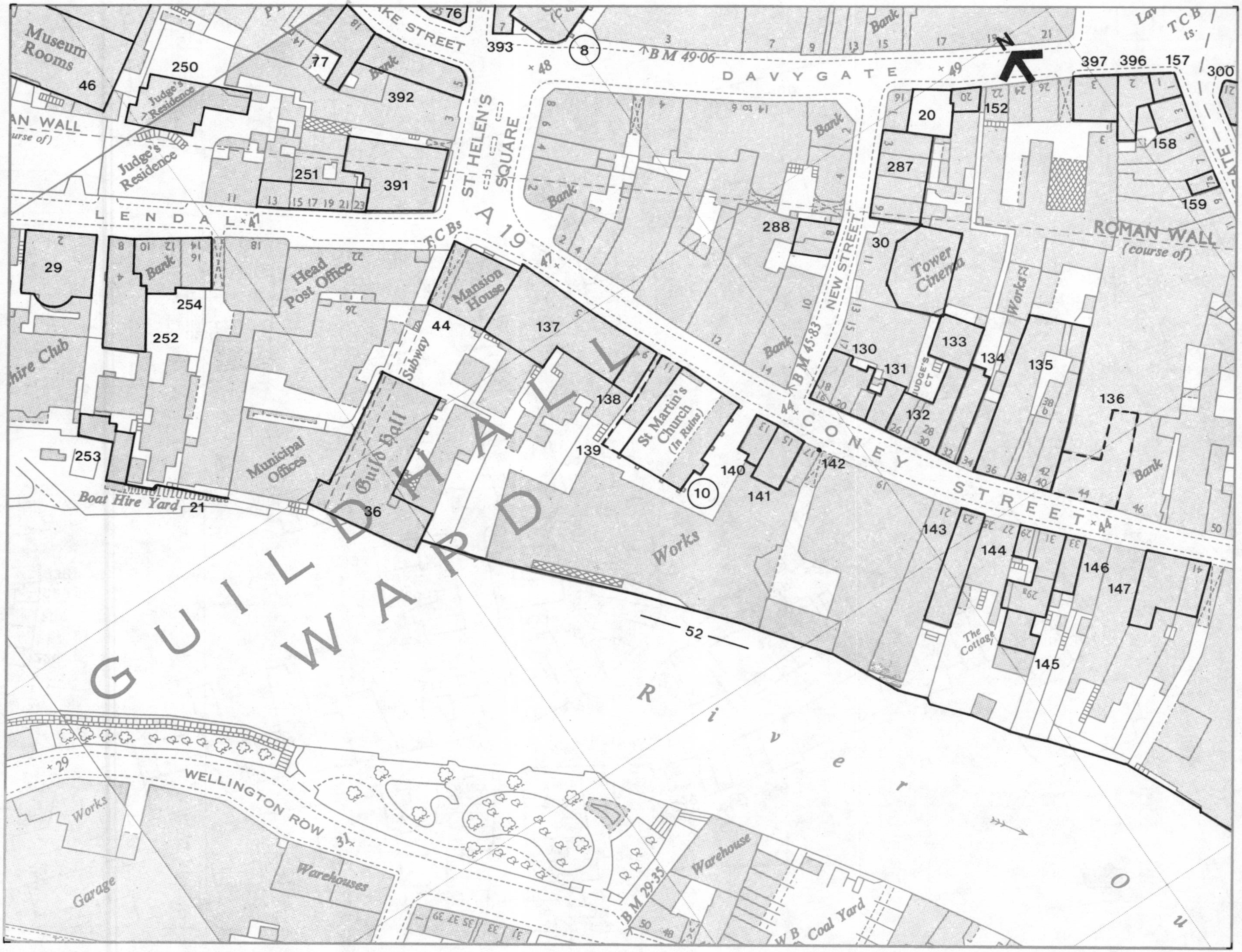

MAP 6. Monuments in the Lendal and Coney Street area.

Scale 1:1250

MAP 7. Monuments in the Ousegate and Castlegate area

Scale 1:1250

MAP 8. Monuments in the Fossgate area.

Scale 1:1250

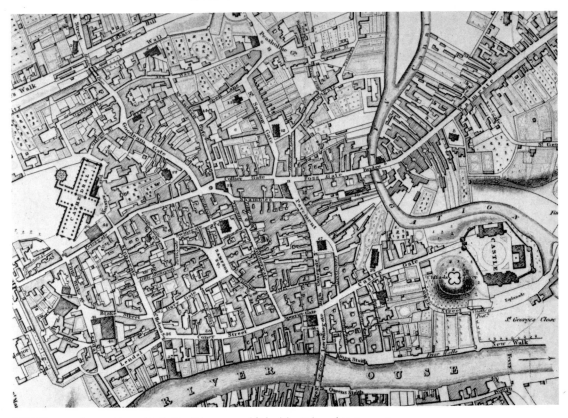

YORK, central area. From *Yorkshire Directory*, published by Edward Baines, 1822.

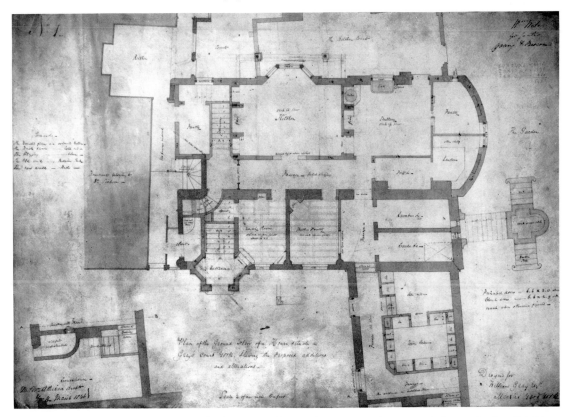

(35) GRAY'S COURT. Ground-floor plan by J. B. and W. Atkinson, 1846 (Messrs. Brierley, Leckenby, Keighley and Groom).

PLATE 2   DRAWINGS OF CHURCHES

(10) ST. MARTIN, CONEY STREET, from N.W.
By W. J. Boddy, 1910 (York City Art Gallery).

(4) ST. CRUX from S.W. From W. Monkhouse and
F. Bedford, *The Churches of York*, c. 1840.

(8) ST. HELEN from St. Helen's Square. By J. C. Buckler, 1816 (Society of Antiquaries), based on his drawing of 1814
(BM, MS. 36396, f. 114).

HOUSE IN MIDDLE WATER LANE (now Cumberland Street), 1778 (Evelyn Collection, © YAYAS).

HABERDASHERS' HALL, WALMGATE. By George Nicholson, 1826 (York City Art Gallery).

FOSSGATE looking S.E. from Pavement. By H. Cave, *c.* 1800 (Evelyn Collection, © YAYAS).

PLATE 4

STREETSCAPES

(409–413) Nos. 16–34 ST. SAVIOURGATE from S.W. 18th-century and later.

(287) CUMBERLAND ROW, Nos. 3–9 New Street, from N.E. 1746.

(337–334) Nos. 35–23.

(333–325) Nos. 21–1.

HIGH PETERGATE, S.W. side.

PLATE 5

PLATE 6 STREETSCAPES

COLLIERGATE, N.E. side.

(193–196) Nos. 41–55 GOODRAMGATE from S.W.

(254, 252) Nos. 14–8 LENDAL from E. *c.* 1714 and later.

(338–341) Nos. 42–54 LOW PETERGATE from S.E.
18th-century and later.

From N.W.
LADY PECKETT'S YARD.

From S.E.

MINSTER GATES from N.E.

COFFEE YARD from S.E.

PLATE 8 AERIAL VIEW

HIGH PETERGATE and PRECENTOR'S COURT from S.E.

(2) HOLY TRINITY, GOODRAMGATE, from S. Mainly 14th and 15th-century.

(10) ST. MARTIN, CONEY STREET, from S.E. 15th-century, reconstructed 1961–8.

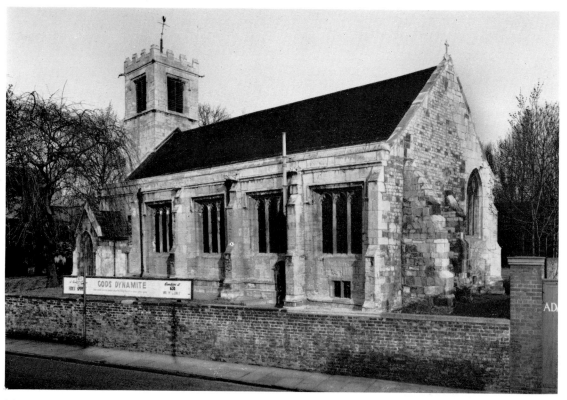

(5) ST. CUTHBERT from S.E. Mainly mid 15th-century.

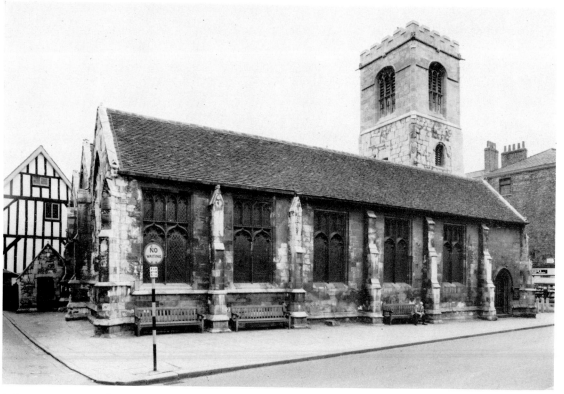

(14) ST. SAMPSON from N. 15th-century, rebuilt 19th century.

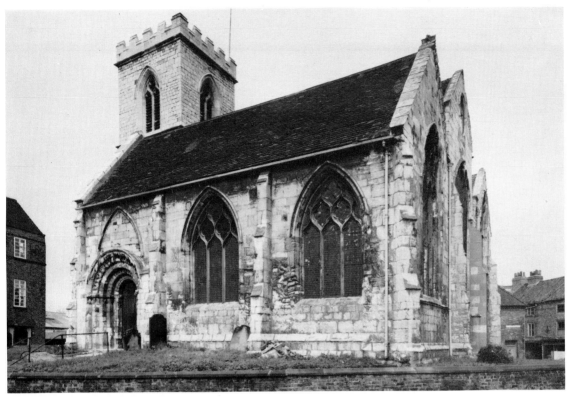

(6) ST. DENYS from S.E. 14th-century and later.

(9) ST. MARGARET from S.E. 14th-century and later.

PLATE 12

CHURCH EXTERIORS

(1) ALL SAINTS, PAVEMENT, from N.W. 14th-century and later.

(15) ST. SAVIOUR from W. 15th-century and later.

PLATE 13

CHURCH EXTERIORS

(8) ST. HELEN from W. Mediaeval, restored 19th century.

(7) ST. GEORGE (R.C.) from S.W. 1850.

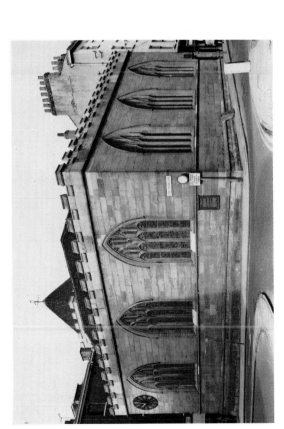

(12) ST. MICHAEL-LE-BELFREY from S.W. 1525–37, restored 19th century.

(13) ST. MICHAEL, SPURRIERGATE, from S.E. Mediaeval and 1821.

PLATE 14   CHURCH EXTERIOR

(11) ST. MARY, CASTLEGATE, from S.E. 10th or 11th-century and later, restored 19th century.

From W.

From E.

(11) ST. MARY, CASTLEGATE. Before alteration in 1974.

(15) ST. SAVIOUR from W. 15th-century and later.

(2) HOLY TRINITY, GOODRAMGATE, from N.E. Mainly 14th and 15th-century.

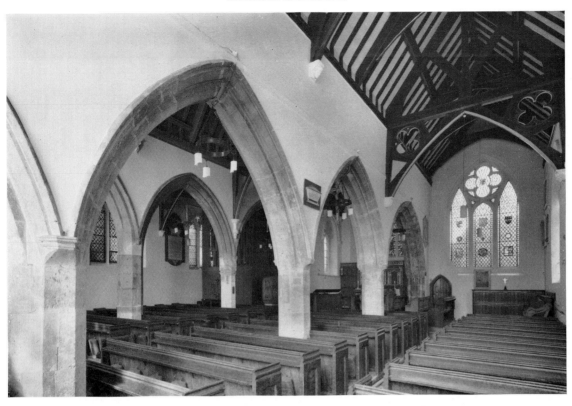

(8) ST. HELEN from S.W. Mediaeval, restored 19th century.

(14) ST. SAMPSON from W., before alteration in 1974. 15th-century, rebuilt 19th century.

PLATE 18

CHURCH INTERIORS

(1) ALL SAINTS, PAVEMENT, from W. 14th-century and later.

(13) ST. MICHAEL, SPURRIERGATE, from S.W. 12th-century and later.

PLATE 19

CHURCH INTERIORS

(12) ST. MICHAEL-LE-BELFREY from N.W. 1525-37.

(10) ST. MARTIN, CONEY STREET. S. aisle from W. 15th-century.

PLATE 20

CHURCH AND CHAPEL: EXTERIORS

(33) BEDERN CHAPEL from N.E., before partial demolition. 14th-century and later.

(3) ST. ANDREW'S HALL from N.W. 15th-century and later.

(40) ST. LEONARD'S HOSPITAL. Cross-shaft fragment (2). Pre-Danish. (Now in Yorkshire Museum).

(6) ST. DENYS. Coped stone (2). 10th or 11th-century.

(40) ST. LEONARD'S HOSPITAL. Cross-shaft fragment (1). Pre-Danish.

(6) ST. DENYS. Grave-slab (1). 10th or 11th-century.

(16) Former BURIAL GROUND. Headstone fragment (3). Pre-Conquest. (Now in Yorkshire Museum).

(11) ST. MARY, CASTLEGATE. Dedication stone (6). 10th or 11th-century.

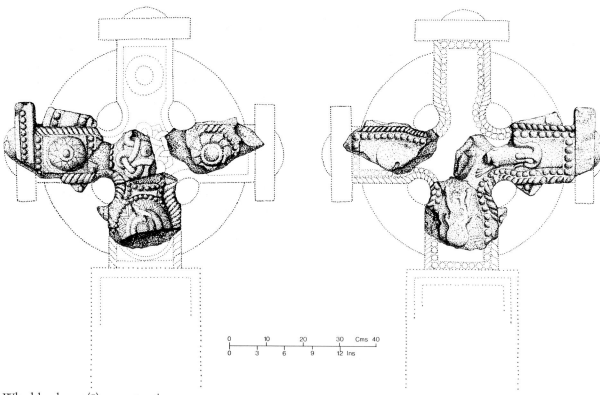

Wheel-head cross (8), reconstruction.

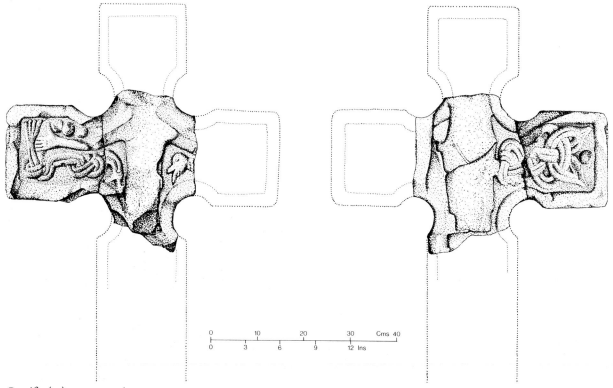

Crucifix (12), reconstruction.

(11) ST. MARY, CASTLEGATE. 10th or 11th-century.

(11) ST. MARY, CASTLEGATE.
Cross-fragment (11). 10th or
11th-century. (Photograph supplied
by York Archaeological Trust).

(289) No. 6 NEWGATE. Cross-shaft fragment. Probably 11th-century.

(1) ALL SAINTS, PAVEMENT.
Coped grave-cover. 10th or early
11th-century.

PLATE 24   CHURCH WINDOWS: 14TH AND 15TH-CENTURY

(2) HOLY TRINITY, GOODRAMGATE. Chapel of
St. James, S. wall. *c.* 1340, reset.

(11) ST. MARY, CASTLEGATE. S. aisle, S. wall.
15th-century.

N. aisle, E. window. *c.* 1350.

(6) ST. DENYS.

S. aisle, E. window. 15th-century.

(11) ST. MARY, CASTLEGATE. N. chapel, W. bay.
Early 14th-century, reset.

(10) ST. MARTIN, CONEY STREET. S. aisle, S. wall.
15th-century.

(6) ST. DENYS. Chancel, E. window. *c.* 1452–55.

(12) ST. MICHAEL-LE-BELFREY. N. aisle, N. wall.
1525–37.

PLATE 26   CHURCH DOORS AND DOORWAYS: 12TH AND 15TH-CENTURY

(9) ST. MARGARET. S. porch. 12th-century, reset from St. Nicholas' Hospital.

(6) ST. DENYS. S. doorway. 12th-century, reset.

(5) ST. CUTHBERT. Door now in S. porch. Mid 15th-century.

(14) ST. SAMPSON. N. door. 15th-century, reset.

Nave, S. arcade. Capital. Late 12th-century.   W. tower. Capital. 15th-century.

(13) ST. MICHAEL, SPURRIERGATE.

Capital and spandrel.   Pier base.

(12) ST. MICHAEL-LE-BELFREY. N. arcade. 1525–37.

PLATE 28

CARVED STONEWORK: 12TH-CENTURY

(6) ST. DENYS. Corbel-heads reset on

(9) ST. MARGARET. Voussoirs of S. porch, details.

(10) ST. MARTIN, CONEY STREET. Voussoirs reset in wall of S. aisle.

PLATE 29

CARVED STONEWORK: LATE 14TH AND 15TH-CENTURY

(11) ST. MARY, CASTLEGATE. S. chapel, E. wall. Angel with shield-of-arms of Graa. Late 14th-century.

Shield-of-arms of Howme.

(2) HOLY TRINITY, GOODRAMGATE. S. aisle, on archway to Chapel of St. James. Early 15th-century.

(4) ST. CRUX PARISH ROOM. Corbel-head reset in S. wall. 15th-century.

Shield.

(10) ST. MARTIN, CONEY STREET. Head on N.E. pier of tower. 15th-century.

(14) ST. SAMPSON. W. tower, S.E. pier. Angel with shield bearing merchant's mark. 15th-century.

PLATE 30

CARVED STONEWORK: 16TH-CENTURY

St. Michael and angels.

God the Father and Christ receiving a soul.

(8) ST. HELEN. N. arcade. Label stops.

PLATE 31

CARVED WOODWORK: 15TH-CENTURY

(5) ST. CUTHBERT. Chancel and nave. Roof bosses.

PLATE 32   ROYAL ARMS AND COMPANY ARMS

Royal Arms of Charles II. 1669.

Arms of Company of Merchant Adventurers. 1765.

(37) MERCHANT ADVENTURERS' HALL. Chapel.

(1) ALL SAINTS, PAVEMENT. Royal Arms. Hanoverian
    before 1801.

(8) ST. HELEN. Royal Arms of George III. 1802.

(1) ALL SAINTS, PAVEMENT. Closing-ring on N. door.

PLATE 34　　　　　　　　　COMMUNION RAILS: 18TH-CENTURY

(12) ST. MICHAEL-LE-BELFREY. By William Etty. 1712.

(2) HOLY TRINITY, GOODRAMGATE. By John Headlam. 1715.

(37) MERCHANT ADVENTURERS' HALL. Chest (1). 13th-century.

(13) ST. MICHAEL, SPURRIERGATE. Chest (2). 17th-century.

Communion Table (1).

(13) ST. MICHAEL, SPURRIERGATE. 17th-century.

Communion Table (2).

(5) ST. CUTHBERT. Communion Table. 17th-century.

(1) ALL SAINTS, PAVEMENT. Communion Table. 17th-century.

PLATE 36

CHURCH FITTINGS: MEDIAEVAL, 17TH AND 18TH-CENTURY

(10) ST. MARTIN, CONEY STREET. Font and cover. Mediaeval and 1717.

(13) ST. MICHAEL, SPURRIERGATE. Door and doorcase (2). Early 18th-century.

(1) ALL SAINTS, PAVEMENT. Pulpit and sounding-board. 1634.

PLATE 37

REREDOSES: 18TH-CENTURY

(13) ST. MICHAEL, SPURRIERGATE. Early 18th-century.

(12) ST. MICHAEL-LE-BELFREY. By William Etty. 1712.

PLATE 38

CHURCH FITTINGS: MISCELLANEOUS

(8) ST. HELEN. Font and bases. Late 12th and 13th-century.

(6) ST. DENYS. Bench-end. 15th-century.

(13) ST. MICHAEL, SPURRIERGATE. Communion rails. Early 18th-century.

Lectern. 15th and 19th-century.

Chair. 17th-century.

(1) ALL SAINTS, PAVEMENT.

(13) ST. MICHAEL, SPURRIERGATE. Chair (1). 17th-century.

PLATE 39

CHURCH FITTINGS: MISCELLANEOUS

(11) ST. MARY, CASTLEGATE. Misericordes. 15th-century.

(13) ST. MICHAEL, SPURRIERGATE. Bells (2–6). 1681 (four) and 1765.

(6) ST. DENYS. Bells. 1718 and 1658.

PLATE 40

BRASSES AND COFFIN LID

(2) HOLY TRINITY, GOODRAMGATE. Coffin lid (2). 13th-century.

(1) ALL SAINTS, PAVEMENT. Brass (6) of Robert Askwith, 1597.

(10) ST. MARTIN, CONEY STREET. Brass (4) of Christopher Harington, 1614.

(10) ST. MARTIN, CONEY STREET. Brass (3) of Thomas Colthurst, 1588.

(2) HOLY TRINITY, GOODRAMGATE. Brass (1) of Thomas Danby, 1458.

(13) ST. MICHAEL, SPURRIERGATE. Brass (2) of William Wilson, d. 1517.

PLATE 41

MONUMENTS: 17TH-CENTURY

(10) ST. MARTIN, CONEY STREET. Monument (4) of Lady Elizabeth Sheffield, 1633. Detail.

(4) ST. CRUX PARISH ROOM. Monument (4) of Sir Robert Watter and detail, 1612.

(6) ST. DENYS. Monument (1) of Dorothy Hughes. Early 17th-century.

(12) ST. MICHAEL-LE-BELFREY. Monument (21) of an infant Vavasour, 1728.

(12) ST. MICHAEL-LE-BELFREY. Monument (25) of Mary Woodyeare, 1728.

(5) ST. CUTHBERT. Monument (5) of Charles Mitley, 1758.

(13) ST. MICHAEL, SPURRIERGATE. Monument (9) of William Hutchinson, 1772.

(4) ST. CRUX PARISH ROOM. Monument (6) of Roger Belwood, 1694.

Monument (2) of Sir Tancred Robinson, 1754.

(4) ST. CRUX PARISH ROOM.

Monument (9) of Henry Waite, 1780.

Plate 44   MONUMENT: 18TH-CENTURY

(12) ST. MICHAEL-LE-BELFREY. Monument (23) of Sir Robert Squire, 1707, and Priscilla his wife, 1711.

Detail from panel 2d.

Heraldry from panels 3b and 3d.

(2) HOLY TRINITY, GOODRAMGATE. Window I. 1471.

PLATE 46   GLASS: 15TH-CENTURY

(2) HOLY TRINITY, GOODRAMGATE.
Window I. Corpus Christi. 1471.

(10) ST. MARTIN, CONEY STREET. Window sIV. Corpus
Christi. Mid 15th-century.

Window I. The Crucifixion. 1452–55.

Window I. The Virgin Mary. 1452–55.

Window sII. Detail. Mid 15th-century.

(6) ST. DENYS.

PLATE 48   GLASS: 14TH-CENTURY

The Entombment.

The Deposition.

The Angel at the Tomb.

The Incredulity of Thomas.

(1) ALL SAINTS, PAVEMENT. Window wI. Late 14th-century.

SS. Peter and Paul.   The Nativity.   The Resurrection.

Window I. Mid 14th-century.

Window nVI. The Virgin of the Annunciation and St. Ursula.   Window sIII. SS. John the Baptist and Peter. 1525–40.
    1525–40.

(12) ST. MICHAEL-LE-BELFREY.

PLATE 50

GLASS: 14TH-CENTURY

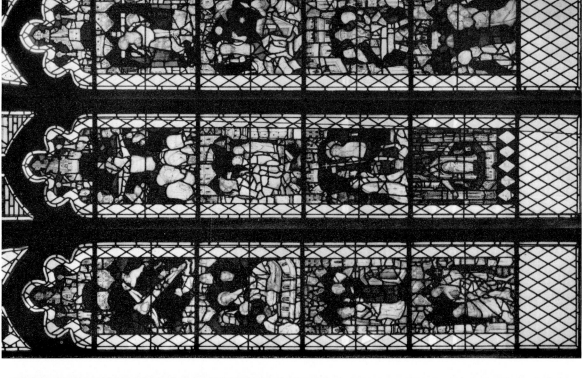

(1) ALL SAINTS, PAVEMENT. Window wI, central lights. Late 14th-century.

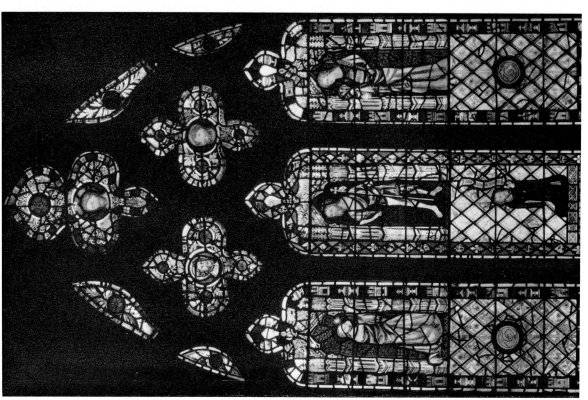

(6) ST. DENYS. Window nIII. Mid 14th-century.

PLATE 51

GLASS: 15TH-CENTURY

(10) ST. MARTIN, CONEY STREET. Window sIV. The Holy Family.
15th-century.

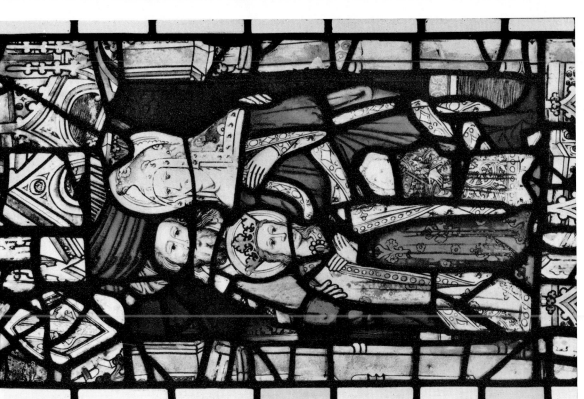

(2) HOLY TRINITY, GOODRAMGATE. Window I. The Holy Family.
15th-century.

PLATE 52

GLASS: 15TH-CENTURY

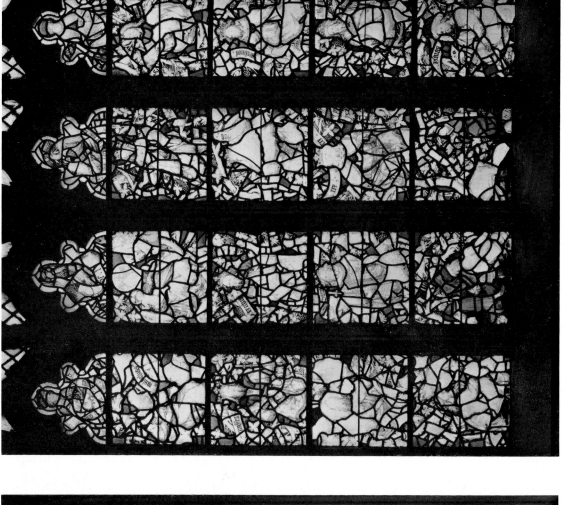

Window sIV. Tree of Jesse. Early 15th-century.

Window sIII. Nine Orders of Angels. First half of 15th century.

(a) ST. MICHAEL SPURRIERGATE

PLATE 53

GLASS: 15TH-CENTURY

Window sV. King and Queen. First half of 15th century.

Window sIV. Isaiah. Early 15th-century.

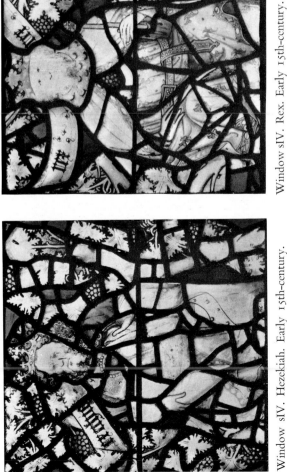

Window sIII. Archangels. First half of 15th century.

Window sIV. Rex. Early 15th-century.

Window sIII. Cherubin. First half of 15th century.

Window sIV. Hezekiah. Early 15th-century.

(13) ST. MICHAEL, SPURRIERGATE.

PLATE 54

GLASS: 15TH-CENTURY

Dominations.

Cherubin.

Donor panel.

(c) ST. MARTIN CONEY STREET. Window: SE. Aisle.

PLATE 55

GLASS: 13TH, 14TH AND 15TH-CENTURY

(2) HOLY TRINITY, GOODRAMGATE. Window nII. The Virgin Mary. c. 1471.

(1) ALL SAINTS. Window wI. Passion shield. Late 14th-century.

(6) ST. DENYS. Window sIII. Angel with symphony. Mid 15th-century.

(6) ST. DENYS. Window nV. Theophilus scenes. Early 13th-century.

PLATE 56   GLASS: 14TH AND 15TH-CENTURY CANOPIES

(12) ST. MICHAEL-LE-BELFREY.   (1) ALL SAINTS, PAVEMENT. Window wI. Late 14th-century.
Window I. Late 14th-century.

Window nII. *c.* 1442.   Window sIV. 15th-century.   (2) HOLY TRINITY,
                                                                                    GOODRAMGATE. Window I. 1471.

(10) ST. MARTIN, CONEY STREET.

St. Christopher.

St. John the Baptist.

St. George.

(2) HOLY TRINITY, GOODRAMGATE. Window I. 1471.

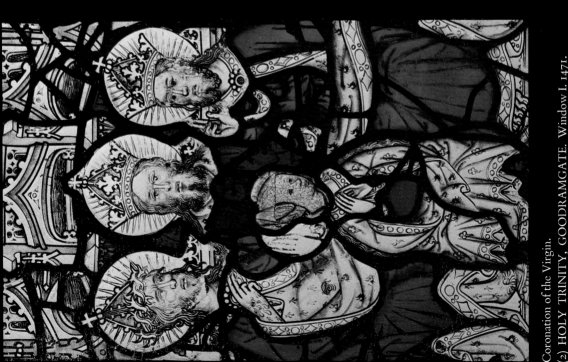

St. Ursula.

Coronation of the Virgin.

(2) HOLY TRINITY, GOODRAMGATE. Window I. 1471.

St. Mary Cleophas, Alphaeus and family.

St. Mary Salome, Zebedee and infant St. John.

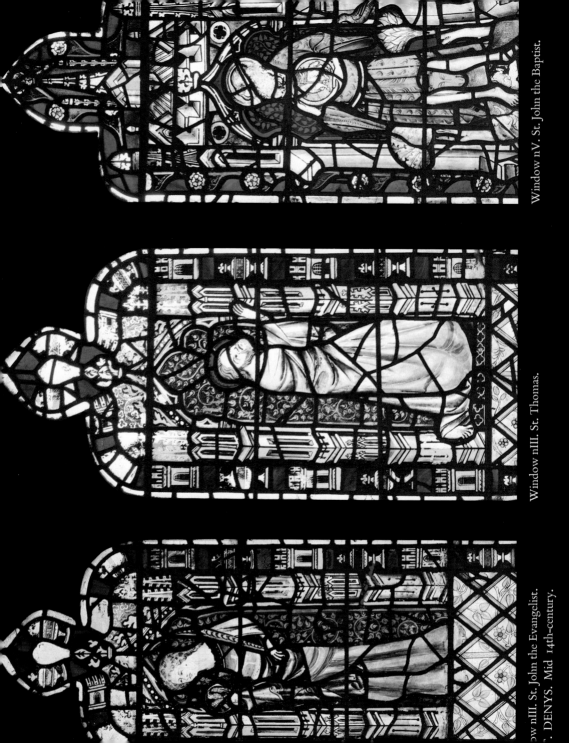

Window nV. St. John the Baptist.

Window nIII. St. Thomas.

ow nIII. St. John the Evangelist.
. DENYS. Mid 14th-century.

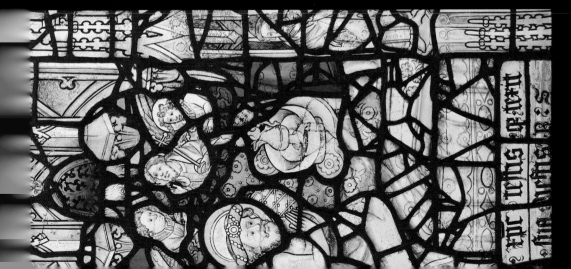

Powers.
Window sIII. First half of 15th century.

Thrones.

Window nV. Scenes from story of Thomas Becket.

Window sV. SS. George and Martin.

(12) ST. MICHAEL-LE-BELFREY. 1525-40.

Window nVI. SS. Michael and Christopher.

PLATE 64 CIVIC PLATE AND SWORD

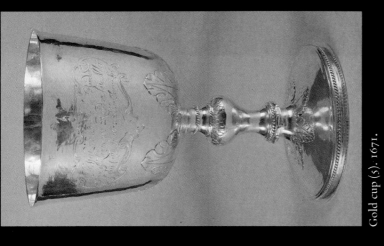

Gold cup (5). 1671.

The Emperor Sigismund's Sword and Scabbard. 1416 and later.

Standing cup (6). 1679.

Centre piece (1). 1796.
(44) MANSION HOUSE.

PLATE 65

Exterior from W.

Interior from S.E.

(33) BEDERN HALL. Mid 14th-century.

PLATE 66 NONCONFORMIST CHAPELS: 17TH AND 19TH-CENTURY

(26) Former EBENEZER PRIMITIVE METHODIST CHAPEL, Little Stonegate. By J. P. Pritchett, 1851.

(31) SALEM CHAPEL. St. Saviourgate. By J. P. Pritchett, 1839.

(32) UNITARIAN CHAPEL, St. Saviourgate. 1692 and later.

(24) CENTENARY METHODIST CHAPEL, St. Saviourgate. By James Simpson, 1840.

(31) SALEM CHAPEL, St. Saviourgate. By J. P. Pritchett, 1839.

(27) FRIENDS' MEETING HOUSE, Clifford Street. By C. Watson and J. P. Pritchett, 1817.

PLATE 68

W. elevation.

Common Hall Lane.

(36) GUILDHALL. *c.* 1449–59.

PLATE 69

Interior from W.

Common Hall Lane.

Common Hall Lane.

(36) GUILDHALL. *c.* 1449–59.

PLATE 70

From N.

From S.

(37) MERCHANT ADVENTURERS' HALL. 1357–61 and later.

PLATE 71

N.E. addition from N. Early 17th-century.

Doorway in N.E. wall of N.E. addition. Early 17th-century.

Doorway in N.E. wall of undercroft. 14th-century.

(37) MERCHANT ADVENTURERS' HALL.

PLATE 72

From S.E.

Interior from N.W.

(37) MERCHANT ADVENTURERS' HALL. Chapel. Early 15th-century and later.

PLATE 73

Great Hall from S.E.

Undercroft. S.W. aisle from N.W.

(37) MERCHANT ADVENTURERS' HALL. 1357–61 and later.

PLATE 74

From S.W.

Interior from S.E.

(38) MERCHANT TAYLORS' HALL. *c.* 1400 and later.

PLATE 75

From S.

Great Hall from N.E.

(39) ST. ANTHONY'S HALL. Mid 15th-century and later.

PLATE 76

From S.W.

Aerial view.

(34) ST. WILLIAM'S COLLEGE. *c.* 1465 and later.

PLATE 77

N. range from S.

W. range from E.

(34) ST. WILLIAM'S COLLEGE. *c.* 1465 and later.

PLATE 78

N. elevation. Stair block. Late 17th-century.

E. range. Oriel window in elevation to courtyard. c. 1465.

(34) ST. WILLIAM'S COLLEGE.

PLATE 79

S. range. Provost's Chamber(?). *c.* 1465.

W. range. Wall-painting. Late 16th-century.

(34) ST. WILLIAM'S COLLEGE.

PLATE 80

N. range. MacLagan Memorial Hall. Formed *c.* 1910.

W. range. Hall at first floor. Formed *c.* 1910.

(34) ST. WILLIAM'S COLLEGE. *c.* 1465.

Drawing Room.

Great Hall.

(35) THE TREASURER'S HOUSE. 17th-century and later; remodelled *c.* 1900.

PLATE 82

S.W. elevation. 1628–48 and later.

Aerial view from S.

(35) THE TREASURER'S HOUSE.

PLATE 83

N.E. elevation. Second half of 16th century and later.

Entrance in S.W. front. 1628–48 and later.

N.E. elevation, S.E. wing. 1628–48.

(35) THE TREASURER'S HOUSE.

PLATE 84   18TH-CENTURY CEILINGS

(35) THE TREASURER'S HOUSE. Dining Room. *c.* 1740.

(35) GRAY'S COURT. Sterne Room. Mid 18th-century.

Queen's Room.

Long Gallery. Entrance to Sterne Room.

South Bedroom.

Sterne Room.

(35) THE TREASURER'S HOUSE AND GRAY'S COURT.

PLATE 86

18TH-CENTURY FITTINGS

Fireplace in West Sitting Room. Mid 18th-century.

Main staircase. c. 1725.

(35) THE TREASURER'S HOUSE.

PLATE 87

18TH-CENTURY FIREPLACES

Dining Room. *c.* 1740 and later.

Drawing Room. Mid 18th-century.

(35) THE TREASURER'S HOUSE.

PLATE 88

MISCELLANEOUS DETAILS

Columns in entrance hall. 12th-century, reset.

W. corner of courtyard. 17th-century and later.

(35) GRAY'S COURT.

PLATE 89

(469) NORMAN HOUSE, behind Nos. 48, 50 Stonegate. Late 12th-century.

PLATE 90

From W.

Undercroft from S.W.

(40) ST. LEONARD'S HOSPITAL, Museum Street. 13th-century.

PLATE 91

(40) ST. LEONARD'S HOSPITAL, Museum Street. Passage from S.W. 13th-century.

PLATE 92   CIVIC SEAL AND MACE

Seal (1) and impressions. 13th-century.

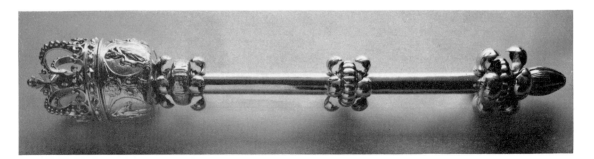

Great Mace. 1647.

(44) MANSION HOUSE.

PLATE 93

(44) MANSION HOUSE. 1726–33.

QUEEN'S GALLERY, SOMERSET HOUSE, from *Vitruvius Britannicus* I (1715), Plate 16.

PLATE 94

Main staircase.

Entrance hall.

(44) MANSION HOUSE. 1726–33.

PLATE 95

(44) MANSION HOUSE. State Room. 1732–33.

PLATE 96

1731–36, refronted by J. P. Pritchett, 1828.

From Drake, *Eboracum* I, 338.

(45) ASSEMBLY ROOMS. Elevation to Blake Street.

PLATE 97

W. wall.

E. wall, detail.

W. wall, detail.

W. wall, detail.

(45) ASSEMBLY ROOMS. Lesser Assembly Room. 1773.

PLATE 98

'Egyptian Hall' from *The Four Books of Andrea Palladio's Architecture*, by Isaac Ware (London, 1738), Second Book, Plate XXVIII.

(45) ASSEMBLY ROOMS. Great Assembly Room from S.W. *c.* 1732.

PLATE 99

Doorway in Circular Room.

Fireplace in Cube Room.

Doorway to Great Assembly Room.

Fireplace in Lesser Assembly Room.

Doorway to N. Front Room.

Fireplace in S. Front Room.

(45) ASSEMBLY ROOMS. c. 1732.

PLATE 100

(48) DE GREY ROOMS, 1841–2, and (394) DE GREY HOUSE, St. Leonard's Place, c. 1835.

PLATE 101

(82) FAIRFAX HOUSE, No. 27 Castlegate. By John Carr, completed 1762.

PLATE 102

(82) FAIRFAX HOUSE, No. 27 Castlegate. Ceiling of Dining Room. *c.* 1762.

PLATE 103

(82) FAIRFAX HOUSE, No. 27 Castlegate. Ceiling of Drawing Room. *c.* 1762.

PLATE 104

Ceiling above main staircase.

Ceiling of stair hall.

(82) FAIRFAX HOUSE, No. 27 Castlegate. *c.* 1762.

PLATE 105

Wall of stair hall.

Wall of main staircase.

Ceiling of N.W. front room, ground floor.

Ceiling of N.W. front room, ground floor.

(82) FAIRFAX HOUSE, No. 27 Castlegate. *c.* 1762.

PLATE 106   18TH-CENTURY CEILINGS

N.W. front room, ground floor.

Saloon.

(82) FAIRFAX HOUSE, No. 27 Castlegate. *c.* 1762.

Entrance hall.

First-floor landing.

Saloon.

Dining Room.

(82) FAIRFAX HOUSE, No. 27 Castlegate. *c.* 1762.

PLATE 108

Window to main staircase.

Main staircase.

(82) FAIRFAX HOUSE, No. 27 Castlegate. c. 1762.

PLATE 109

Rear elevation.

Front elevation.

(89) CASTLEGATE HOUSE, No. 26 Castlegate. By John Carr, 1762–3.

PLATE 110

Secondary staircase.

Main staircase.

(89) CASTLEGATE HOUSE, No. 26 Castlegate. 1762–3.

PLATE 111

Doorway in Drawing Room.

Fireplace in Drawing Room.

Doorway in Saloon.

Doorway in S.W. room, ground floor.

Fireplace in S.W. room, ground floor.

(89) CASTLEGATE HOUSE, No. 26 Castlegate. 1762–3.

PLATE 112

Stair hall.

Front elevation.

(417) PEASHOLME HOUSE, St. Saviour's Place. 1752.

PLATE 113

Main entrance.

Front elevation.

(250) THE JUDGE'S LODGING, No. 9 Lendal. Early 18th-century.

PLATE 114

(250) THE JUDGE'S LODGING, No. 9 Lendal. Window to main staircase. Early 18th-century.

PLATE 115

Fireplace in entrance hall.

Fireplace in Breakfast Room.

Main staircase.

First-floor passage.

(250) THE JUDGE'S LODGING, No. 9 Lendal. Early 18th-century.

PLATE 116

(50) FOSS BRIDGE from S.W. By Peter Atkinson junior, 1811.

(240) WHITE ROSE CAFE, Jubbergate. 14th and early 17th-century.

(222) LADY ROW, Nos. 60–72 Goodramgate. *c.* 1316 and later.

PLATE 118   TIMBER-FRAMED BUILDINGS

(519) RED LION p.h., Merchantgate. 15th-century and later.

(537) BOWES MORRELL HOUSE, No. 111 Walmgate. *c.* 1400 and later.

(130) Nos. 16–22 CONEY STREET. 15th or early 16th-century and later.

(215) Nos. 30, 32 GOODRAMGATE. 14th-century and later.

PLATE 120

TIMBER-FRAMED BUILDINGS

(299) Nos. 16, 18, 20 OGLEFORTH. 16th-century.

(174) QUEEN'S HEAD p.h., No. 44 Fossgate. Late 15th-century.

(478) MULBERRY HALL, Nos. 17, 19 Stonegate. Mid 15th-century and later.

(311) HERBERT HOUSE, Nos. 12, 14 Pavement. Early 17th-century.

PLATE 122

TIMBER-FRAMED BUILDINGS

(193) Nos. 41, 43, 45 GOODRAMGATE. Late 15th or early 16th-century and later.

(307) BUILDING IN PATRICK POOL. Late 16th-century.

PLATE 123

TIMBER-FRAMED BUILDINGS

Front Range.

Hall Range.

(194) Nos. 49, 51 GOODRAMGATE. Late 15th or early 16th-century.

PLATE 124

TIMBER-FRAMED BUILDINGS

(437) Nos. 37, 38 SHAMBLES. Late 15th-century.

SHAMBLES from N.W.

PLATE 125

STREETSCAPES

LOW PETERGATE from S.E.

STONEGATE from N.E.

PLATE 126   TIMBER-FRAMED BUILDINGS

(317) THE BLACK SWAN p.h., Peasholme Green. Late 16th-century and later.

(536) No. 77 WALMGATE. 15th-century and later.

(222) No. 64 GOODRAMGATE. Roof truss. *c.* 1316.

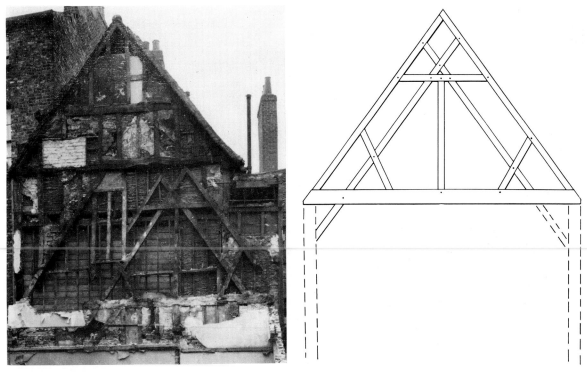

Before demolition.   Reconstruction.

(131) BUILDING BEHIND NO. 24 CONEY STREET. Roof truss. Late 13th or early 14th-century.

PLATE 128

TIMBER-FRAMED BUILDINGS: HALLS

(194) No. 51 GOODRAMGATE. Late 15th or early 16th-century.

(193) No. 45 GOODRAMGATE. Late 15th or early 16th-century.

PLATE 129

TIMBER-FRAMED BUILDINGS: INTERIORS

Former Hall. First floor, E. wall.

E. wing. First floor, N.E. room.

(537) BOWES MORRELL HOUSE, No. 111 Walmgate. c. 1400.

PLATE 130   TIMBER-FRAMING DETAILS

(222) No. 70 GOODRAMGATE. First-floor room. *c.* 1316.

(436) No. 35 SHAMBLES. Roof truss. Late 14th-century.   (420) No. 7 SHAMBLES. Roof truss. Late 15th-century.

(488) No. 35 STONEGATE. 15th-century.

(193) No. 45 GOODRAMGATE. Front range. Late 15th or early 16th-century.

PLATE 132   TIMBER-FRAMING DETAILS

Central truss.

S.W. wall.

(485) No. 2 COFFEE YARD. Former hall. 15th-century.

(174) QUEEN'S HEAD p.h., No. 44 Fossgate. Late 15th-century.

(37) MERCHANT ADVENTURERS' HALL. Great Hall, N.E. aisle. 1357–61.

PLATE 134

TIMBER-FRAMING DETAILS

Roof detail. Early 14th-century.

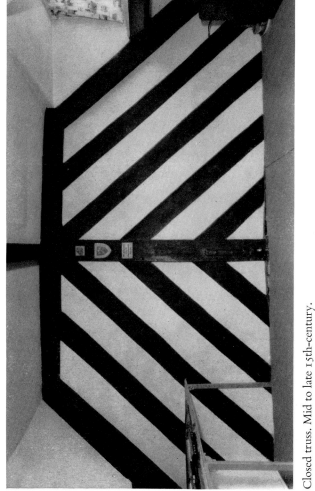

Closed truss. Mid to late 15th-century.

Roof bosses. Mid to late 15th-century.

PLATE 135

TIMBER-FRAMING DETAILS

(530) No. 45 WALMGATE. E. gable. 14th-century.

(436, 437) Nos. 35 and 37 SHAMBLES from W. Late 14th and late 15th-century.

(291) No. 15 NEWGATE. S.W. end. 1337.

PLATE 136

18TH-CENTURY GABLES

(335) Nos. 25, 27, 29 HIGH PETERGATE. c. 1700.

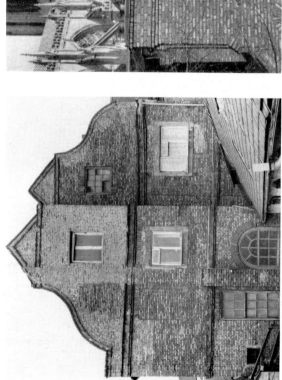

(164) Nos. 13, 14 FOSSGATE. c. 1720.

(200) No. 81 GOODRAMGATE. Early 18th-century.

(85) No. 12 CASTLEGATE. c. 1730.

(375) Nos. 2, 3, 4, 4a PRECENTOR'S COURT. Early 18th-century.

PLATE 138   18TH-CENTURY HOUSES

(249) CUMBERLAND HOUSE, No. 9 King's Staith. *c.* 1710.

(61) OLIVER SHELDON HOUSE, Nos. 17, 19 Aldwark. *c.* 1720.

(156) THE RED HOUSE, Duncombe Place. Early 18th-century.

(277) THE OLD RESIDENCE, No. 6 Minster Yard. Second quarter of 18th century.

PLATE 140   18TH-CENTURY HOUSES

(411) No. 26 ST. SAVIOURGATE. c. 1725.

(344) No. 62 LOW PETERGATE. c. 1725.

(115) Nos. 15, 16 COLLIERGATE. Mid 18th-century.

(133) JUDGES' COURT, behind Nos. 28, 30 Coney Street. Early 18th-century.

(410) No. 24 ST. SAVIOURGATE. c. 1763.

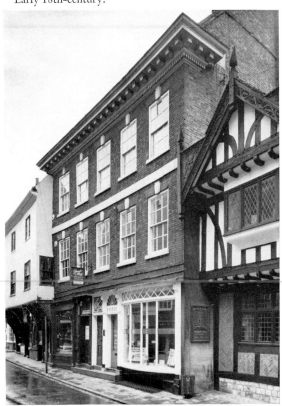

(474) No. 9 STONEGATE. c. 1740–50.

(316) Nos. 26, 28 PAVEMENT. *c.* 1700.

(319) No. 4 HIGH PETERGATE. 1782.

(416) No. 14 ST. SAVIOUR'S PLACE. *c.* 1775.

(280) No. 10 MINSTER YARD. 1753–5.

(74) Nos. 15–21 BLAKE STREET. 1773.

(76) No. 25 BLAKE STREET. 1785.

(383) No. 20 ST. ANDREWGATE. Late 18th-century.

(157, 158) Nos. 1 and 3 FEASEGATE. 1770.

PLATE 144

18TH-CENTURY HOUSES

(233) Nos. 11, 12 HIGH OUSEGATE. c. 1705.

(296) CROMWELL HOUSE, No. 13 Ogleforth. c. 1700, gable rebuilt c. 1974.

(234) Nos. 13, 14 HIGH OUSEGATE. Early 18th-century.

PLATE 145

18TH-CENTURY HOUSES

(275) No. 4 MINSTER YARD. Early 18th-century.

(378) No. 10 PRECENTOR'S COURT. Early 18th-century.

PLATE 146

18TH-CENTURY HOUSES

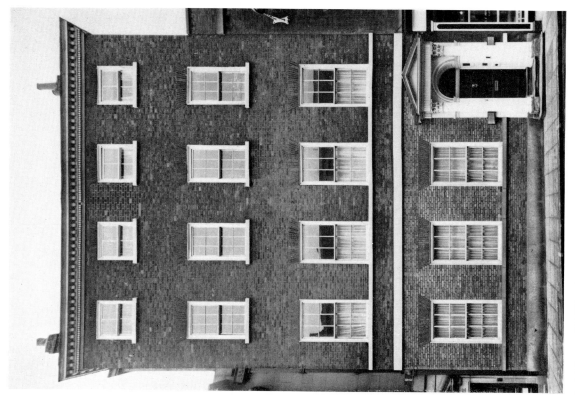

(77) No. 18 BLAKE STREET. c. 1789.

(477) No. 15 STONEGATE. 15th-century, refronted mid 18th century.

PLATE 147

18TH-CENTURY HOUSES

(334) No. 23 HIGH PETERGATE. *c.* 1779.

(397) MELROSE HOUSE, No. 3 St. Sampson's Square. Late 18th-century.

PLATE 148

GARDEN ELEVATIONS

(378) No. 10 PRECENTOR'S COURT from N.E. Mediaeval, early 18th-century and later.

(35) GRAY'S COURT from N.E. 14th, 18th and 19th-century.

(480) No. 23 STONEGATE from S. 16th and 17th-century and later.

(91) No. 8 CHAPTER HOUSE STREET from N.E. Early 18th-century and later.

PLATE 149

18TH AND 19TH-CENTURY HOUSES

(390) Nos. 48, 50 ST. ANDREWGATE. 1824–30.

(387) No. 42 ST. ANDREWGATE. c. 1740.

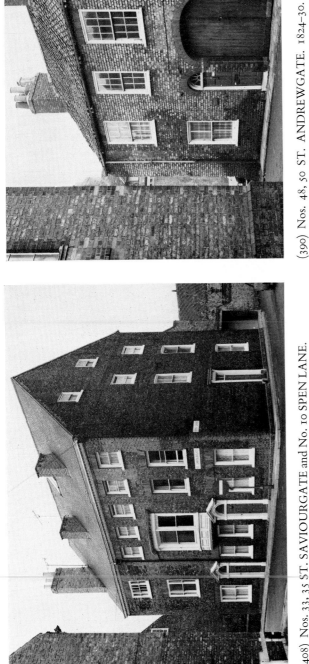

(408) Nos. 33, 35 ST. SAVIOURGATE and No. 10 SPEN LANE. c. 1770–80.

(181) Nos. 9–17 GEORGE STREET. c. 1842.

PLATE 150

Front elevation. 1830–33.

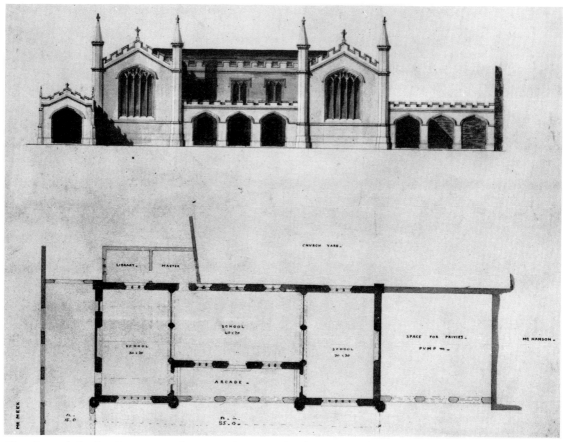

Elevation and plan by C. Watson and J. P. Pritchett, 1830 (York Minster Library).

(49) THE MINSTER SONG SCHOOL.

PLATE 151

N.E. elevation. *c.* 1837.

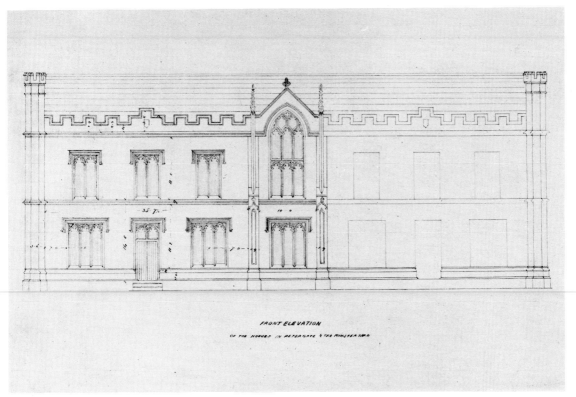

FRONT ELEVATION

Elevation by J. P. Pritchett, 1837 (York Minster Library).

(279) Nos. 8, 9 MINSTER YARD.

PLATE 152   19TH-CENTURY BUILDINGS

(41) LADY HEWLEY'S HOSPITAL, St. Saviourgate. By J. P. Pritchett, 1840.

(154) PUREY-CUST CHAMBERS, Dean's Park. By R. H. Sharp, 1824–5.

(42) DOROTHY WILSON'S HOSPITAL, No. 2 Walmgate. 1812.

(392) YORK COUNTY SAVINGS BANK, No. 5 St. Helen's Square. By Watson, Pritchett and Watson, 1829–30.

PLATE 154

From S.E. Begun 1834.

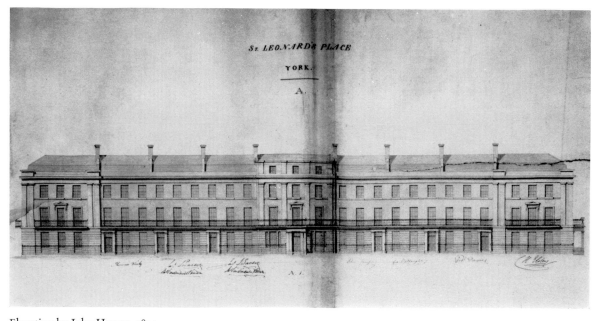

Elevation by John Harper, 1834.

(395) Nos. 1–9 ST. LEONARD'S PLACE.

(391) No. 1 ST. HELEN'S SQUARE. By G. T. Andrews, 1846–7.

(301) MIDLAND BANK, No. 13 Parliament Street. By P. F. Robinson and G. T. Andrews, 1835.

PLATE 156   19TH-CENTURY BUILDINGS

(285) MIDLAND BANK, No. 1 Nessgate. By J. B. and W. Atkinson, 1839.

(352) Nos. 37, 39 LOW PETERGATE, 1827–8.

(451) Nos. 4–22 SPURRIERGATE. *c.* 1841.

(405) MASONIC HALL, St. Saviourgate. By J. B. and W. Atkinson, 1845–6.

(490) No. 37 STONEGATE. Early 19th-century.

(467) No. 46 STONEGATE. Early 19th-century.

PLATE 158   15TH-CENTURY DOORS AND DOORWAYS

(38) MERCHANT TAYLORS' HALL. Door and doorway to screens passage. 15th-century.

(34) ST. WILLIAM'S COLLEGE. Original entrance door. c. 1465.

(4) ST. CRUX PARISH ROOM. Door (1). Early 15th-century.

(36) GUILDHALL. Main doorway. Mid 15th-century.

(61) OLIVER SHELDON HOUSE, Nos. 17, 19 Aldwark. *c.* 1720.

(249) CUMBERLAND HOUSE, No. 9 King's Staith. *c.* 1710.

(296) CROMWELL HOUSE, No. 13 Ogleforth. *c.* 1700.

(411) No. 26 ST. SAVIOURGATE. *c.* 1725.

PLATE 160   18TH-CENTURY DOORWAYS

(334) No. 23 HIGH PETERGATE. *c.* 1779.

(275) No. 4 MINSTER YARD. Late 18th-century.

(407) No. 29 ST. SAVIOURGATE. Late 18th-century.

(340) No. 52 LOW PETERGATE. 1772.

(205) No. 3 MONK BAR COURT. Early to mid
19th-century.

(410) No. 24 ST. SAVIOURGATE. Early 19th-century.

(383) No. 20 ST. ANDREWGATE. Late 18th-century.

(301) MIDLAND BANK, No. 13 Parliament Street. 1835.

PLATE 162   DOORWAYS

(174) QUEEN'S HEAD p.h., No. 44 Fossgate. First floor. Late 17th-century.

(275) No. 4 MINSTER YARD. First floor, N.W. room. Early 18th-century.

From Hall. 15th-century; door 18th-century.

From Committee Room. 1680.

(36) GUILDHALL. Doorway between Hall and Committee Room 1.

(35) GRAY'S COURT. Sterne Room.
    Mid 18th-century.

(287) No. 7 NEW STREET. First
    floor, front room. 1746.

(287) No. 3 NEW STREET. First
    floor, back room. 1746.

(254) No. 10 LENDAL. Saloon. Late
    18th-century.

(483) No. 31 STONEGATE. First
    floor, front room. Late 18th-century.

(154) PUREY-CUST CHAMBERS,
    Dean's Park. First floor. 1824–5.

(137) No. 5 CONEY STREET. Ground floor. (From photograph in Yorkshire Museum).

(131) No. 24 CONEY STREET. Second floor, front room.

(137) No. 7 CONEY STREET. First floor, back room. *c.* 1600.

PLATE 166

17TH-CENTURY PLASTERWORK: CEILINGS

(61) OLIVER SHELDON HOUSE, Nos. 17, 19 Aldwark. Rear block, ground-floor room. Early 17th-century.

(270) No. 2 MINSTER COURT. Room N.W. of entrance hall. Early 17th-century.

PLATE 167

18TH-CENTURY PLASTERWORK: CEILINGS

(249) CUMBERLAND HOUSE, No. 9 King's Staith. Above staircase. c. 1710.

(254) No. 10 LENDAL. Above staircase. c. 1714.

PLATE 168

18TH-CENTURY PLASTERWORK: CEILINGS

(344) No. 62 LOW PETERGATE. Above main staircase. *c.* 1725.

(61) OLIVER SHELDON HOUSE, Nos. 17, 19 Aldwark. Above staircase. *c.* 1720.

(45) ASSEMBLY ROOMS. Recess to Great Assembly Room. *c.* 1732.

PLATE 169

18TH-CENTURY PLASTERWORK: CEILINGS

(89) CASTLEGATE HOUSE, No. 26 Castlegate. Drawing Room. 1762–3.

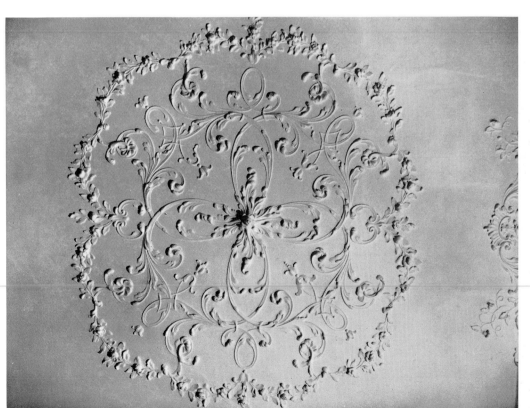

(270) No. 1 MINSTER COURT. Music Room. Mid 18th-century.

PLATE 170   17TH-CENTURY PANELLING

(317) THE BLACK SWAN p.h., Peasholme Green. Smoke Room. Early 17th-century, reset.

(471) No. 58 STONEGATE. First floor, front room. Early 17th-century.

(249) CUMBERLAND HOUSE, No. 9 King's Staith. Ground floor, N.W. room. *c.* 1710.

(516) No. 70 WALMGATE. First floor, W. room. Early 18th-century.

PLATE 172   18TH-CENTURY PANELLING

(147) No. 39 CONEY STREET. S.E. house. Second floor, front room. *c.* 1710–20.

(375) No. 4 PRECENTOR'S COURT. Ground floor, front room. Early 18th-century.

(409) No. 18 ST. SAVIOURGATE. Ground floor, back room. *c.* 1740.

(147) No. 39 CONEY STREET. N.W. house. Saloon. Mid 18th-century.

PLATE 174

17TH AND EARLY 18TH-CENTURY FIREPLACES

(346) THE FOX INN, Low Petergate. *c.* 1600.

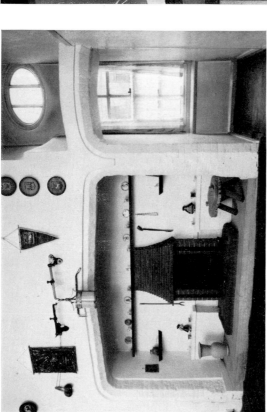

(35) THE TREASURER'S HOUSE. Kitchen. 17th-century.

(37) MERCHANT ADVENTURER'S HALL. Great Hall, S.W. aisle. Early 18th-century.

(311) HERBERT HOUSE, Nos. 12, 14 Pavement. First floor, front room.

(480) No. 23 STONEGATE. Central Block, first floor.

EARLY 17TH-CENTURY OVERMANTELS

PLATE 176   18TH-CENTURY FIREPLACES AND OVERMANTELS

(287) No. 3 NEW STREET. First floor, back room. 1746.

(287) No. 7 NEW STREET. First floor, front room. 1746.

(287) No. 7 NEW STREET. Ground floor, front room. 1746.

(277) No. 6 MINSTER YARD. Ground floor, back room. Second quarter of 18th century.

(117) No. 19 COLLIERGATE. Saloon. 1748.

(516) No. 70 WALMGATE. First floor, E. back room. Mid 18th-century.

Plate LXXXVI.   Plate LXXX.

Designs from Batty Langley, *The City and Country Builder's and Workman's Treasury of Design* (1745).

PLATE 178   18TH-CENTURY FIREPLACES AND OVERMANTELS

(312) HOUSE at S. end of LADY PECKETT'S YARD. N. wing, second floor. Early 18th-century.

(156) THE RED HOUSE, Duncombe Place. First floor, S. room. Early 18th-century.

(249) CUMBERLAND HOUSE, No. 9 King's Staith. Ground floor, S.W. room. *c.* 1710.

(232) No. 5 HIGH OUSEGATE. First floor, E. room. 1743.

(472) No. 3 STONEGATE. First floor, front room. Second quarter of 18th century.

(77) No. 18 BLAKE STREET. First floor, E. room. *c.* 1789.

(44) MANSION HOUSE. First floor, S.W. room. Late 18th-century. (From Adelphi Buildings, London).

(147) No. 39 CONEY STREET. N.W. house. First floor, back room. *c.* 1800.

(275) No. 4 MINSTER YARD. Ground floor, S.E. room. Late 18th-century.

(35) GRAY'S COURT. Bow-fronted room. 1846.

PLATE 180

18TH AND 19TH-CENTURY FIREPLACES

(492) No. 45 STONEGATE. Saloon.   Second quarter of 18th century.

(287) No. 9 NEW STREET. Second floor, back room. 1746.

(483) No. 31 STONEGATE. First floor, front room. Late 18th-century.

(278) No. 7 MINSTER YARD. Ground floor, N.E. room. Early 19th-century.

(378) No. 10 PRECENTOR'S COURT. First floor, N.E. room. Second quarter of

(480) No. 23 STONEGATE. 1590.

(61) Nos. 17, 19 ALDWARK, 1732.

(80) No. 7 CASTLEGATE. 1789.

(233) No. 11 HIGH OUSEGATE. 1758.

(232) No. 5 HIGH OUSEGATE. 1743.

(410) No. 24 ST. SAVIOURGATE. 1763.

(358) Nos. 59, 61 LOW PETERGATE. c. 1763.

(340) No. 52 LOW PETERGATE. 1772.

(254) No. 10 LENDAL. Bracket. c. 1714.

PLATE 182

MISCELLANEA

(41) LADY HEWLEY'S HOSPITAL. Tablet on Warden's House. 1700, reset.

(36) GUILDHALL. Doorway in W. wall.

(42) DOROTHY WILSON'S HOSPITAL. Tablet at first floor. 1812.

(36) GUILDHALL. Committee Room 1. Stuart

(38) MERCHANT TAYLORS' HALL. Tablet on Hospital. 1730.

This Hospital and School House were endowed by Mrs Dorothy Wilson Spinster, for the Maintenance of ten poor Women as also for the Instruction in English Reading Writing and Clothing of twenty poor Boys for ever She departed this Life the 3rd of November 1717

(42) DOROTHY WILSON'S HOSPITAL. Tablet at second floor. 18th-century, reset.

(156) THE RED HOUSE, Duncombe Place.

PLATE 183

12TH, 13TH AND 14TH-CENTURY WINDOWS

(40) ST. LEONARD'S HOSPITAL, Museum Street. Undercroft, S.W. wall. 13th-century.

(35) GRAY'S COURT. Entrance hall, N.W. wall. 12th-century.

(469) NORMAN HOUSE. S.W. wall. Late 12th-century.

(37) MERCHANT ADVENTURERS' HALL. Undercroft, S.W. wall. 1357–61.

Exterior.

Interior.

(33) BEDERN CHAPEL. E. wall. Possibly late 13th-century.

PLATE 184

17TH-CENTURY WINDOWS

(480) No. 23 STONEGATE. W. wing, S.W. wall.

(485) No. 2 COFFEE YARD. S.E. block, N.E. wall.

(216) No. 38 GOODRAMGATE. Rear elevation.

PLATE 185

(312) HOUSE at S. end of LADY PECKETT'S YARD. N. elevation.

(484) No. 1 COFFEE YARD. N.E. wall.

(297) THE DUTCH HOUSE, No. 2 Ogleforth. Front elevation. (Photo. Northern Echo).

(528) No. 25 WALMGATE. Rear elevation.

(35) THE TREASURER'S HOUSE. N.E. elevation.

(527) No. 23 WALMGATE. Building at rear. N.E. wall.

PLATE 186   18TH-CENTURY GLASS

(38) MERCHANT TAYLORS' HALL. Little Hall. S.W. window. By Henry Gyles, 1700–2.

(488) No. 35 STONEGATE. By William Peckitt. Second half of 18th century. (Now in York City Art Gallery).

(38) MERCHANT TAYLORS' HALL. Little Hall.
N.W. window. By Henry Gyles, *c.* 1700.

(287) No. 9 NEW STREET. Staircase window.

(36) GUILDHALL. Stuart Royal Arms. By Henry Gyles. (By courtesy of the Victoria and Albert Museum).

PLATE 188   SCREENS PASSAGE AND ENTRANCE HALLS

(38) MERCHANT TAYLORS' HALL. Screens passage.
c. 1400.

(317) THE BLACK SWAN p.h., Peasholme Green.
Entrance passage. Late 17th-century.

(344) No. 62 LOW PETERGATE. Entrance hall. c. 1725,
altered c. 1770.

(327) No. 5 HIGH PETERGATE. Entrance hall. Early
19th-century.

(488) No. 35 STONEGATE. Top flight. *c.* 1700 with early
17th-century balusters, reset.

(345) No. 64 LOW PETERGATE. 'Talbot stairs'. Mid to
late 17th-century.

(317) THE BLACK SWAN p.h., Peasholme Green.
Late 17th-century.

(312) HOUSE at S. end of LADY PECKETT'S YARD.
N. wing. Late 17th-century.

PLATE 190   18TH-CENTURY STAIRCASES

(375) No. 4a PRECENTOR'S COURT. Early
18th-century.

(288) No. 8 NEW STREET. *c.* 1745, with earlier balusters
reset.

(249) CUMBERLAND HOUSE, No. 9 King's Staith.
Back stair. *c.* 1710.

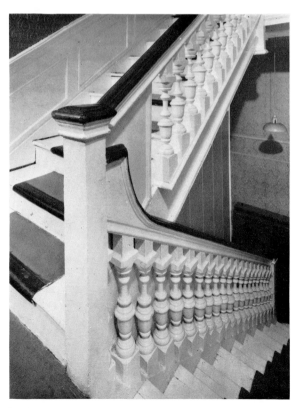

(133) JUDGES' COURT, Coney Street. Main stair. Early
18th-century.

(249) CUMBERLAND HOUSE, No. 9 King's Staith.
Main stair. *c.* 1710.

(254) No. 10 LENDAL. *c.* 1714.

(407) No. 31 ST. SAVIOURGATE. Probably 1735.

(516) No. 70 WALMGATE. Early 18th-century.

PLATE 192   18TH-CENTURY STAIRCASES

(287) No. 9 NEW STREET. 1746.

(287) No. 7 NEW STREET. 1746.

(277) No. 6 MINSTER YARD. Second quarter of 18th century.

(480) No. 23 STONEGATE. N.E. hall. c. 1750.

(280) No. 10 MINSTER YARD. 1753–5.

(296) CROMWELL HOUSE, No. 13 Ogleforth. *c.* 1760.

(77) No. 18 BLAKE STREET. *c.* 1789.

(147) No. 39 CONEY STREET. N.W. house. Mid 18th-century.

(154) PUREY-CUST CHAMBERS, Dean's Park. 1824–5.

(480) No. 23 STONEGATE. W. wing. Second quarter of 19th century.

(395) No. 3 ST. LEONARD'S PLACE. c. 1834.

(395) No. 5 ST. LEONARD'S PLACE. c. 1834.

(395) No. 6 ST. LEONARD'S PLACE. c. 1834.

(395) No. 1 ST. LEONARD'S PLACE. *c.* 1834.

(395) No. 7 ST. LEONARD'S PLACE. *c.* 1834.

From Walker pattern book. (Now in Castle Museum, York).

(279) No. 8 MINSTER YARD. 1837.

PLATE 196

18TH-CENTURY STAIRCASES

(344) No. 62 LOW PETERGATE. c. 1725.

(334) No. 23 HIGH PETERGATE. c. 1779.

PLATE 197

CARVED WOODWORK

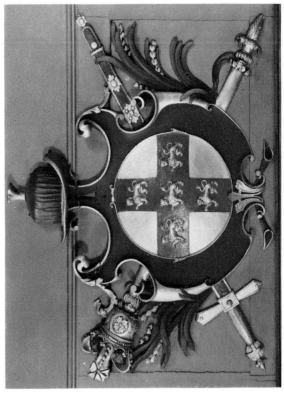

(36) GUILDHALL. Committee Room 1. Inscription, 1679, and City Arms, probably 1762.

(44) MANSION HOUSE. State Room. City Arms above fireplace. 1732–3.

(471) No. 58 STONEGATE. First floor, front room. Early 17th-century.

(344) No. 62 LOW PETERGATE. Door on half-landing, centre panels. 16th-century.

PLATE 198

CARVED WOODWORK

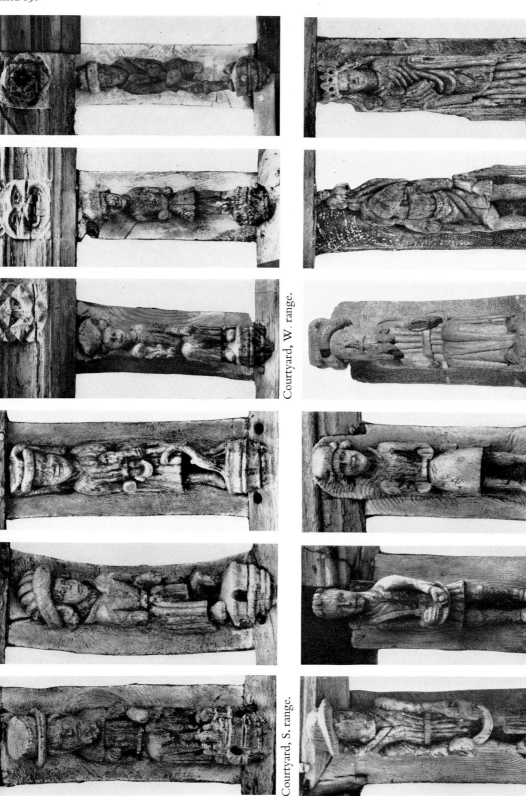

Courtyard, S. range.

Courtyard, N. range.

Courtyard, W. range.

Courtyard, E. range.

Figure now in Yorkshire Museum

Virgin and Child.

St. Christopher.

PLATE 199

CARVED WOODWORK

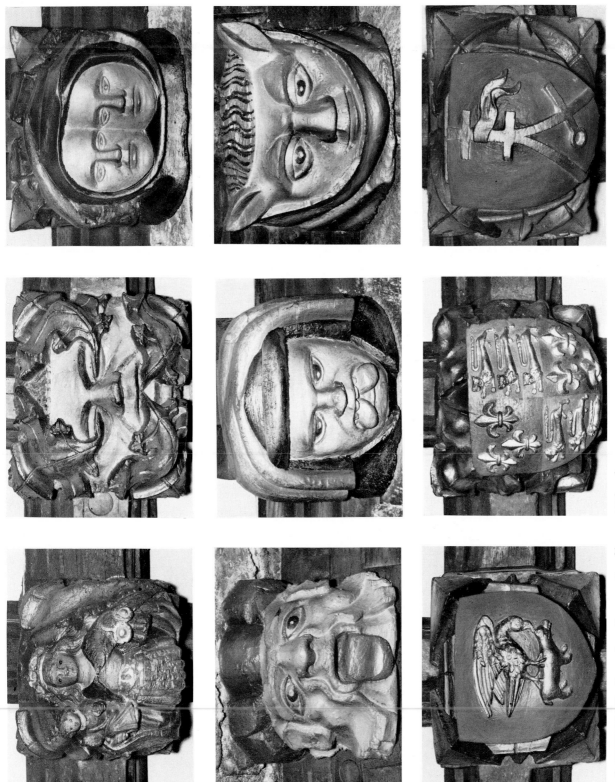

(36) GUILDHALL. Committee Room 1. Roof bosses. Mid 15th-century.

PLATE 200   DOORWAYS AND STAIRCASE DETAILS

(438) No. 37 SHAMBLES. Late 15th-century.

(485) No. 2 COFFEE YARD. 15th-century.

(377) FENTON HOUSE, No. 9
Precentor's Court. Early
18th-century.

(61) OLIVER SHELDON HOUSE,
Nos. 17, 19 Aldwark. c. 1720.

(344) No. 62 LOW PETERGATE.
c. 1725.